HD

2004

Stretch!

Stretch!

How Great Companies Grow in Good Times and Bad

Graeme K. Deans

Fritz Kroeger

WILEY

John Wiley & Sons, Inc.

Published by John Wiley & Sons, Inc., Hoboken, New Jersey.
Published simultaneously in Canada.

For general information on our other products and services please contact our
Customer Care Department within the United States at (800) 762-2974, outside the
United States at (317) 572-3993 or fax (317) 572-4002.

Wiley also publishes its books in a variety of electronic formats. Some content that
appears in print may not be available in electronic books. For more information
about Wiley products, visit our web site at www.wiley.com.

Library of Congress Cataloging-in-Publication Data:

Deans, Graeme K.
   Stretch! : how great companies grow in good times and bad / Graeme K.
Deans, Fritz Kroeger.
      p.   cm.
   Includes bibliographical references and index.
   ISBN 0-471-46893-2 (CLOTH)
   1. Corporations—Growth.   2. Industrial management.   3. Business
   cycles.   I. Kroeger, Fritz.   II. Title.
HD2746.D43   2003
658.4′06—dc22

                                                                    2003015160

Printed in the United States of America.

10   9   8   7   6   5   4   3   2   1

To my wife, Julia, my children, Benjamin and Penelope, and my mother, Barbara, with all my love.

G. K. D.

To my three ladies: Almuth, Carolin, and Isabel.

F. K.

Contents

PART I

THE GROWTH LANDSCAPE

PART II

THE CASE FOR GROWTH

PART III

THE STRETCH GROWTH MODEL

CHAPTER 9 141

CHAPTER 10 159

PART IV

EXECUTION AND CONCLUSION

CHAPTER 11 179

PREFACE

Growth—it was important for the companies that were part of the nineteenth-century industrial revolution. The new technology of mass production enabled it. The robber barons thrived on it as they stretched their rail lines, their oil exploration, their banking empires. In this, the third century of the modern corporation, growth is still the mantra and mission of every company. Visit a company web site. Attend an annual meeting or listen to a securities analyst. Read an annual report or a corporate history. The company's past and future growth is a fundamental topic.

Growth is not a buzzword. Nor is it a new management technique. That lack of newness makes it no less important for every company. The strategy and tactics for growth may change with every era, with changes in exogenous factors, but they are always rooted in a combination of daredevil strategy and solid execution.

We embarked on this book because we believe passionately that companies in the twenty-first century have forgotten how to grow or are too risk-averse to make it happen. Our work on two earlier books, *Winning the Merger Endgame* and *The Value Growers,* convinced us that much rich material about corporate growth is embedded in A.T. Kearney's ongoing research. So we decided to forge ahead and uncover it. *Stretch!* is the result.

GRAEME K. DEANS
FRITZ KROEGER

ACKNOWLEDGMENTS

Writing a book in the management consulting environment is a highly collaborative effort. Many of our colleagues contributed ideas, examples, and insights. We thank all of them but especially these supportive and unselfish souls:

- The global strategy team at A.T. Kearney shared their leading-edge thinking on growth. In particular, we want to thank Tim MacDonald, Joseph Crepaldi, Mike Reopel, Art Bert, Jeff Perry, Jamil Satchu, Steve Manacek, and Bruno Montmerle. Gillis Jonk and Dolf Balkema also shared their work on value chain reconfiguration.

- Reviewing our nearly complete manuscript and providing valuable input, ideas, comments, and suggestions were Jim McDonnell, John Egan, and Paul Laudicina.

- We thank our European colleagues for their great partnership in bringing these new concepts to market. We could not have done this without the invaluable insights of Werner Kreuz, Berthold Hannes, Peter Pfeiffer, Thomas Rings, Joachim Rotering, Ingo Willems, Robert Kremlicka, Thomas Kratzert, Peter C. Allan Andersen, Svein Olaf Engenes, Pablo Gomez Martinez, and especially Jürgen Rothenbücher, Nikolaus Schumacher, Peter Behner, and Roberto Crapelli.

- Stefan Zeisel, as always, provided broad and valuable input and research insights. We appreciate Dirk Pfannenschmidt's ongoing commitment in testing endless new hypotheses and theorems and Nancy Shepherd's and Karen Miske's support with the research. Anja Mainzer was endlessly patient in typing somewhat chaotic manuscript tapes.

■ Most of all, our writing team of Lee Anne Petry, Stefan Zeisel, and Nancy Bishop made this project a reality. Lee Anne was our editorial quarterback and succeeded in getting the manuscript produced and expedited. Nancy, our project manager, monitored our schedule and the arcane elements of book creation at A.T. Kearney.

■ We also appreciate the work of our editor Matthew Holt of John Wiley & Sons for marshaling the resources necessary to bring this project to fruition.

G.K.D.
F.K.

INTRODUCTION

THE POSSIBILITIES OF GROWTH

Today's best business leaders obsess about growth. For years, they focused relentlessly on operational excellence, reengineering, restructuring, and cost reduction. But lately, a new way of thinking has emerged. Believing they have completed the process of reshaping their companies, executives realize that efficiency, cost effectiveness and operational excellence are not the panaceas they thought. They have engaged in an endless pursuit of top-line growth, determined to exploit their companies' potential to generate long-term shareholder value.

Yet, despite the savvy and success of a handful of leaders, many other leaders are not well versed in the business of stretching and growing. Many leaders fear taking the dramatic steps—and risks—needed to lead their companies to exponential growth. They think improving efficiency and reducing costs are low risk, while growth initiatives carry a high risk. Other CEOs believe growth is influenced so strongly by the external business cycle that they have no direct control over their own destiny.

They are wrong.

Over the past three years, A.T. Kearney has conducted numerous studies on both the short- and long-term corporate growth. Using a database that encompasses 98 percent of the world market capitalization, we have examined 29,000 firms over 14 years in addition to interviewing CEOs during various briefings. With this information in hand, we arrived at some key conclusions:

1. Growth is possible in any industry, in any region, in any phase of the business cycle: There is no excuse for not growing.

2. Growth is driven predominantly by eight internal drivers, covering soft and hard factors, across operations, structure, and strategy.

3. As strategic innovation is only one of many growth levers, most growth initiatives have a low level of risk.

4. The barriers to growth are different for every company, and, as a result, the path to growth is equally unique.

5. Long-term growth is the decisive driver of stock prices, thus companies are in control of their own stock price destiny.

6. All industry consolidation follows a similar pattern that includes four distinct stages; a successful long-term strategy must master each one through appropriate growth initiatives.

During 2002, we conducted executive briefings on various strategic topics with active and potential clients—mainly CEOs, CFOs, and corporate strategists. We got input from nearly 1,000 executives in Europe, North America, and Asia. (Approximately 78 percent of them were European and 22 percent non-European.) Our executive attendees received handheld voting devices for answering questions, which provided the participants with immediate consolidated results, starting with the question, "To what extent does your company exploit its growth potential?" The results were amazing: More than half felt that their company was only moderately reaching its true growth capability (see Figure I.1).

This is where our journey begins.

THE GROWTH STUDIES

This book is based on decades of A.T. Kearney client experience and many years of research on corporate growth. We first consider what we know about the importance and process of growth. A.T. Kearney has conducted two major, long-term studies that

FIGURE I.1   HOW WELL DOES YOUR COMPANY EXPLOIT ITS
GROWTH POTENTIAL?

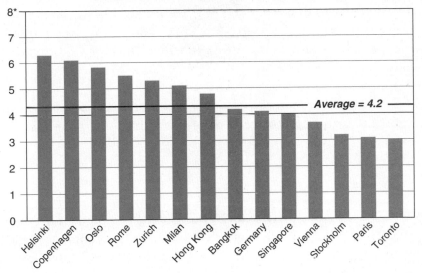

Note: 8 = High score.
Source: Survey of 953 senior leaders from A.T. Kearney executive briefings from 1999 to 2003.

provide insight into the question of corporate success: the Value-Building Growth Study and the Merger Endgames Analysis.

We embarked on the Value-Building Growth Study in 1998 by creating a database of more than 29,000 companies that covered 98 percent of the world market capitalization. With this type of coverage and with a 14-year trend analysis capability, it was possible for the first time to test hypotheses on virtually all of the stock exchange-listed companies in the global economy.

From this database, A.T. Kearney investigated and gained an understanding of the characteristics of successful growth. We analyzed these companies worldwide over a 10-year period, covering 24 major industries in 34 countries and including more than 80 in-depth case studies. In addition, our consultants interviewed more than 80 CEOs and senior executives of leading companies including Bayer, Ericsson, Federal Express, General Electric, Gehe, Mitsubishi Chemical, Norsk Hydro, and Sprint.

The final analysis challenged traditional thinking about the way growth should be viewed and understood. It revealed an attractive kind of growth that we called *Value-Building Growth*. Conscious pursuit of Value-Building Growth has helped a select group of companies create levels of shareholder value above and beyond what conventional, complacent, or profit-oriented companies generate and far beyond the returns of companies that grow merely for growth's sake.

The A.T. Kearney Growth Matrix

We evaluated growth attributes by positioning companies on a two-by-two matrix with value growth on the x- or horizontal axis and revenue growth on the y-axis (see Figure I.2). We calculated value

FIGURE I.2   THE A.T. KEARNEY GROWTH MATRIX

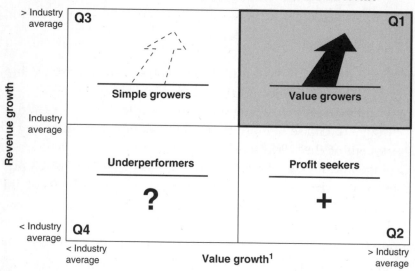

[1] Measured as adjusted market capitalization growth = Market capitalization growth adjusted for change in equity.

Source: James McGrath, Fritz Kroeger, and Michael Traem, *The Value Growers* (New York: McGraw-Hill, 2000).

as a company's stock price with adjustments in equity. In turn, this gave us adjusted market capitalization (AMC). We used the growth of AMC to track value growth rather than revenue growth, the most commonly used measure of growth for a corporation.

Using the growth matrix, four distinct categories of companies emerged:

1. *Value growers:* Companies that outperform their peers in revenue and value growth to achieve the dominant position.

2. *Profit seekers:* Companies that have above-average value growth but are lagging behind in revenue growth.

3. *Simple growers:* Companies that place a strong emphasis on revenue but don't deliver on the value axis.

4. *Underperformers:* The "dogs" of growth—companies that are underperforming in revenue and in value growth.

Uprooted Assumptions

As we analyzed patterns of growth and performance, we found our assumptions overturned time after time, like trees in a windstorm:

- *Industry maturity:* We toppled assumptions about differences between young and mature industries and their respective growth rates and performance. We found high-performing companies in very old industries such as retail and poorly performing companies in new high-tech industries. There is no such thing as a mature industry; there is only mature management.

- *Geography:* We found that geographic location is not a significant factor in growth and stock performance. Both strong and poor performers are located in all regions.

- *Business cycle:* Strong growth (and the related increase in stock price) does not just happen during positive business cycles. We found companies with solid results and corresponding stock prices during economic downturns and poor performers during economic booms.

In other words, strong and successful growth is possible in any industry in any region during any phase of the business cycle.

The Foundations of Value

We also found that a rise in share price is closely linked to long-term growth—and not to other financial indicators such as economic value added (EVA), economic earnings (EE), or cash flow return on investment (CFROI). We found a strong, long-term correlation across all companies in our database between revenue growth and shareholder value growth.

We then took a closer look at companies in the value-growers quadrant of the matrix to learn the hidden secrets behind their obvious success. We found that their executives differ dramatically from leaders of the companies in the other three quadrants in their mind-set—one that focuses on innovation, risk taking, and aggressiveness. Value growers never waver in their focus on innovation, regardless of the economic climate, and they are keenly aware that continually improving products and springboarding into "white space" opportunities are essential to securing future sales growth. Value growers also depend heavily on geographic expansion for growth, rather than focusing solely on exploiting market growth in familiar markets.

Looking at how this growth was achieved, we found that successful companies traditionally pursued a combination of internal (organic, incremental) and external (merger and acquisition) growth. The commonly held belief that acquisitions, more than internal efforts, lead to successful, growing companies does not hold true. In fact, in our group of value growers, 87 percent of their growth was derived from internal activities, compared with 13 percent from external drivers.

Growing Up through Mergers and Acquisitions

The necessity for external growth leads companies to make acquisitions that aren't always the best fit. Studies have shown that many mergers do not result in the value intended. In 1999, A.T. Kearney research showed that half of all mergers or acquisitions failed to increase shareholder value. It seemed clear that a better understanding of successful merger activity was imperative to overall value growth and business success. After years of observing and working on mergers and acquisitions, we undertook analyses that became the foundation for A.T. Kearney's Merger Endgame Model.

To carry out this analysis, we drew from databases that tracked more than 135,000 mergers and acquisitions from 1990 to 1999. We selected publicly traded companies that were quoted on national exchanges with deals worth at least US$500 million in which the acquirer held at least a 51 percent interest at the close of the deal. This led us to focus on 1,345 mergers and acquisitions by 945 acquiring companies. These data were then compared against our Value-Building Growth database. Given the scope and depth of the combination of these parameters, this was the first time that this type of data on the global industrial economy was available in a single body of work.

All Industries Consolidate and Follow a Similar Course

We tracked the change in industry concentration over time using the metric CR3, defined as the market share of the three largest players in an industry. We found that, in all cases, it takes approximately 25 years for an industry to commence, deconsolidate, consolidate, and balance out. As Figure I.3 illustrates, this activity pattern forms an S-curve with four discrete stages on the way to inevitable global consolidation:

1. *Opening:* Little or no market concentration occurs and the first consolidations may appear. Newly deregulated, start-up, and spin-off subsidiaries occupy this space.

2. *Scale:* Size begins to matter. Major players begin to emerge and take the lead in consolidation. Concentration rates can be as high as 45 percent in some industries.

FIGURE I.3   THE MERGER ENDGAMES S-CURVE

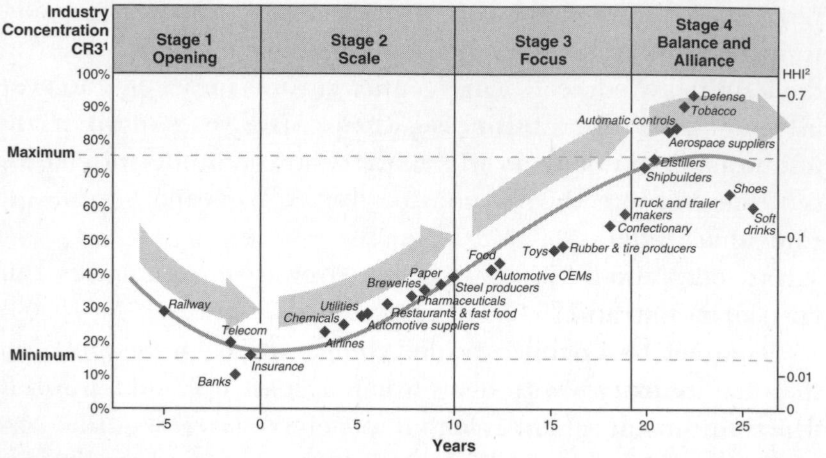

[1] CR3 = Market share of the three largest companies of the total market based on Value-Building Growth database (29,000 companies).
[2] HHI = Hirschman-Herfindahl Index corresponds to the sum of the squared market shares of all companies and is greater than 90 percent—the axis logarithmically plotted.
Source: Graeme K. Deans, Fritz Kroeger, and Stefan Zeisel, *Winning the Merger Endgame* (New York: McGraw-Hill, 2003).

3. *Focus:* Successful players extend their core businesses, exchange or eliminate secondary units, and continue to aggressively outgrow the competition.

4. *Balance and alliance:* A few players will dominate the industry, with consolidation rates as high as 90 percent. Industry titans reign, from tobacco to automotive companies and engine producers. Large companies may form alliances with other giants because growth at this stage is more challenging.

Each stage implies specific strategic and operational imperatives. Knowing and following these imperatives will position a firm well in growing and establishing value. When we dug deeper, we found that long-term successful companies had obviously followed this approach. Exxon, Alcoa, John Deere, Diageo, Philip Morris, Procter & Gamble, General Electric, and Pfizer have clearly and intentionally consolidated their industries. Less successful companies, including Bayer, Deutsche Bank, General Motors, IBM, and AT&T, have followed different paths.

Using the Endgames Curve, future industry consolidation can be predicted. What was surprising to us was that the speed of consolidation does not differ much across industries. Extrapolating the trends observed from the past 13 years into the future indicates that it takes an industry at the bottom of the Endgames Curve today about 20 years to move into the highest level of industry concentration, the balance and alliance stage.

This may be a drastic change from history. For example, the shipyard industry has been around for 4,000 years and is still at the beginning of the balance and alliance stage. The automotive industry is more than 100 years old and is just reaching the end of the scale stage. It will likely need another 10 to 13 years to move into the balance and alliance stage.

Why has it taken so long to move along the curve in the past—and why is the timing contracting? The heart of the answer lies in a functioning global market intertwined with a capital market. Globalization drives industry consolidation, which is significant for all corporations in all industries in all regions. In today's global economy, companies must prepare for consolidation and carry it out well to deliver value-based growth and remain viable.

SCALING THE GROWTH SUMMIT

Given that long-term revenue growth drives shareholder value and that industry consolidation is inevitable, a firm must use these tools to remain a successful, viable entity. There are no exceptions. A firm must grow—and to grow, a firm must pursue consolidation during the appropriate stage on the Endgames Curve.

Specifically, because we can predict the merger activity in an industry and because each stage on the Endgames Curve is associated with specific strategic and operational imperatives, this curve can be used as a road map to guide a company as it develops a strategic viewpoint about growth and consolidation.

Set time frames for consolidation mean that a corporation's strategic horizon must stretch well beyond the ordinary two or three years. The schedule is no longer mentally unlimited—it is clearly defined according to the firm's position on the Value-Building Growth Matrix and the Merger Endgames Curve.

Value-Building Growth is the imperative for success and survival. If we think back to our panel of business leaders who all had growth on their minds, a question arises. Why, with the potential for growth being a recognized opportunity, are there still such barriers to growth? We asked this audience a follow-up question: What are your main barriers to growth? Participants were provided with options that were both internal and external. Aggregated results confirmed that internal, cultural barriers are not the only issues corporations face. In fact, the responses highlighted severe deficiencies throughout the entire value chain. These deficiencies were often obvious problems that could be solved to provide enormous benefit for the corporation and the industry. These problems *must* be addressed by future value growers (see Figure I.4).

Realizing growth possibilities on an individual, national, or even global scale would nearly double the global growth rate. Companies that realized their growth potential would increase their profits, depending on the utilization rate of their fixed assets, by 40 percent to 60 percent and would see their stock valuation rise by 50 percent to 100 percent. On a broader scale, in this Utopia, national unemployment rates would drop by 1 percent to 2 percent, states could reduce taxes, and governments could increase investments in education and scientific research.

The companies that view Value-Building Growth as crucial and aggressively maintain focus on this often-difficult objective are the future winners of their industries. This book builds on the Value-Building Growth Matrix and the Merger Endgames Curve to provide a tangible, growth-focused approach that is relevant to all companies in all industries in all countries.

FIGURE I.4   WHAT ARE THE MAIN BARRIERS TO GROWTH?

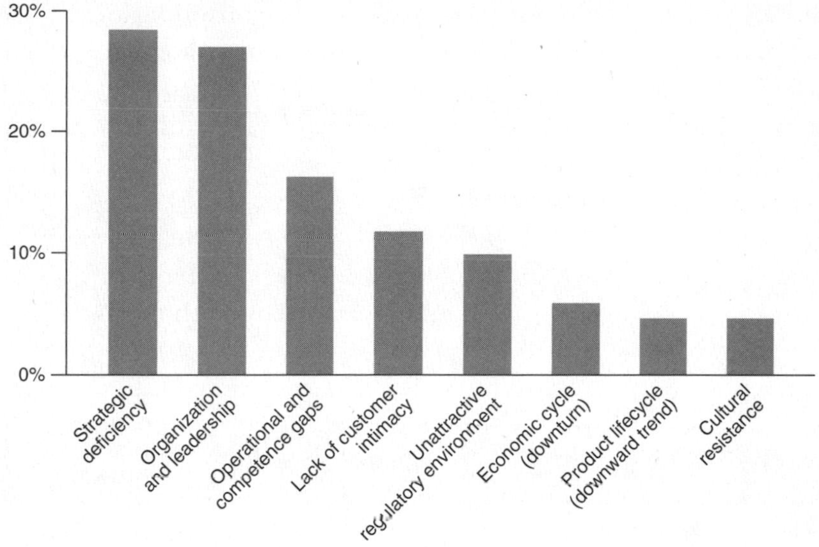

Source: Survey of 953 senior leaders from A.T. Kearney executive briefings from 1999 to 2003.

MAXIMIZING IMPACT: THE STRETCH GROWTH MODEL

Migrating through the four steps of the growth model can lead companies to new levels of business performance. The stages are ordered to provide maximum business impact as quickly and easily as possible while avoiding exposure to huge amounts of risk. Some risk, however, is unavoidable (see Figure I.5).

We describe these four steps to growth in detail in later chapters:

1. *Operations.* The foundational step, requires the company to clean its operational house until it shines, concentrating on dramatic improvements in internal processes such as product development, sourcing, quality, delivery, customer service, sales, and pricing.

FIGURE I.5 THE STRETCH GROWTH MODEL

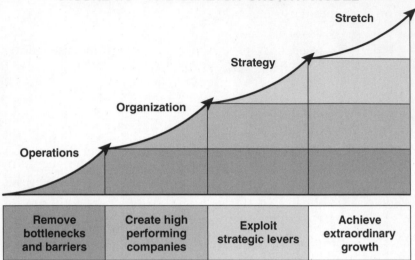

Source: A.T. Kearney.

2. *Organization.* The step where the company works on organizational structure, including its hierarchies of reporting and responsibility. This process involves finding the most appropriate organizational structure (how business units and geographies are organized and relate to each other), determining opportunities for value chain reconfiguration, as well as evaluating and adjusting compensation, reward, and incentive systems.

3. *Strategy.* Involves the most common approach to growth: reinventing, redesigning, and reshaping the core strategy and brand of the firm. This step requires focusing on the value proposition offered to the customer, brand stretch, or line extension. Although executives often leap into this step first, a new strategy will never be truly successful if the first two foundational steps are ignored.

4. *Stretch.* Expanding the business frontier, occurs when the company ventures into new territory, strategically and geographically. The stretch model can have a powerful effect,

breaking down old barriers to create new products for new markets, new customer bases, and new geographies.

We illustrate each of these steps with intriguing case studies from our client experiences and other sources.

GETTING THE MOST OUT OF THIS BOOK

In Part I, we describe the current growth dilemma for the many corporations that find their growth has flat-lined. We ask why this is so and look at why existing approaches to growth and tools for measuring it have failed. We also discuss how governments, which might provide an environment in which business could flourish (provide jobs, create wealth, and pay taxes into the government treasury), have instead hindered growth more than they have helped it.

In Part II, we make the case for growth. The key message of the section is that companies that don't grow have a limited future. The meat of these chapters explores various growth patterns, helps executives determine where their companies fit, and provides strategies on gearing up for growth.

In Part III, we discuss the four growth steps and describe examples of companies that have succeeded (or failed) at growth.

Finally, in Part IV, we describe some approaches to execution—making the stretch model of growth work. We recommend how to leverage the Value-Building Growth Matrix and look at various implementation considerations.

In the final chapter of the book, we summarize our conclusions and walk out on some limbs to predict the future of corporate growth.

PART I

THE GROWTH LANDSCAPE

CHAPTER 1

Mapping the Challenges and Hurdles to Growth

Growth is a universal mandate for business leaders. Every CEO talks about it. Every annual report highlights it. Every equity analyst values share prices based on it. The term *blue chip* refers to a company that seems to have an impenetrable growth model—sustainable, profitable organic growth creation in both good times and bad—that makes it a foolproof investment.

But the conclusions we've drawn from our research, and the focal point of this book, show a different picture. Growth was easy to come by in the boom times of the 1990s. But when the market soured, there was a subtle, yet perceptible, shift in how executives approached the issue of growth. The rhetoric among CEOs stayed the same, but the actions behind the words slowed to a standstill. In a down market, few seem willing to invest in creating a growth engine for their companies. Or, when faced with a tough quarter, growth projects invariably rise to the top of the funding casualty list. Although this helps to achieve short-term cost-cutting gains and hold the share price steady, it sacrifices long-term growth. Another common misstep is to obfuscate growth by pursuing ill-conceived and poorly executed mergers.

Many of these tactics filter down from the top, where compensation packages effectively encourage this behavior, for better or, often, for worse. Most packages, for example, penalize CEOs for investing in growth and force them to resort to short-term profit improvement programs. Although this approach maximizes the value of stock options, it leads to cost cutting by throttling back on longer term value creation necessities such as product development and brand building. This mind-set often works for a year or two, but over a longer period, it virtually guarantees that competitiveness, growth, and shareholder value will be destroyed.

In this chapter, we examine the state of growth as it is perceived—and misperceived—among today's top executives and their companies. We begin the discussion with one of the most telling findings of our research: CEOs confess they are able to realize just 50 percent of the growth potential of the firms they lead. A 50 percent success rate is a number that no executive is satisfied with, and the fact that it's now the norm offers little consolation. This performance gap, as disconcerting as it may be, represents a huge opportunity for potential increases in share prices, as well as in the economic development and wealth creation capabilities of nations. Taking advantage of this opportunity begins with finding the answers to some key questions: Why is it so difficult to overcome the barriers to growth? Why are directors, executives, business advisors, and management consultants so much less successful in implementing *growth* than they are in bringing about efficiency improvements, reducing costs, and reengineering business processes?

THE GROWTH CHALLENGE: IT'S MORE THAN ONE SUMMIT

Want proof that growth is the biggest management challenge in business today? Do you need to be convinced that growth is hard to come by? Look at the plight of four companies—all global leaders, flagship components of the prestigious Dow Jones Industrial

Average (DJIA), and synonymous with growth. The only problem: They aren't growing.

1. *Procter & Gamble:* A global consumer products powerhouse, Procter & Gamble (P&G) is often cited as the world's leading marketing and brand management company and is a mainstay example in classrooms and books, including Tom Peters' blockbuster *In Search of Excellence.* In the late 1990s, P&G's growth engine propelled it to Asia, where the company made aggressive moves into the high-growth markets of China and Southeast Asia. Despite its efforts, P&G grew at a rate of just 2.4 percent compounded between 1997 and 2002. This is slower than the U.S. economy, which grew at a rate of almost 3 percent.

2. *International Business Machines:* Under the helm of CEO Lou Gerstner, Big Blue achieved what many consider to be the most successful—and highest profile—corporate turnaround ever. Gerstner stormed into new markets, including business consulting and software solutions, made several large acquisitions, and created significant internal growth engines. Yet its growth rate between 1997 and 2002 was only 2.4 percent— the same as P&G and just as far behind the growth rate of the U.S. economy.

3. *Coca-Cola:* Surely Coca-Cola, the world's most recognized brand, enjoys stellar growth rates. A marketing powerhouse and the dominant soft drink in both mature and emerging markets, Coca-Cola is also one of the largest equity holdings of Warren Buffett, the legendary stock market guru. But Coca-Cola also faces growth challenges. Between 1997 and 2002, it grew at a rate of 3.3 percent.

4. *Disney:* Finally, there's Disney, the global entertainment powerhouse. From movies and television to theme parks and retail stores, Disney is everywhere there are children—and parents seeking to keep their feisty offspring amused. In recent years, Disney has gone global, opening theme parks in

Europe and Asia. But although the company's reach has expanded, its growth rates have not: From 1997 to 2002, Disney grew at just 0.7 percent.

Some might argue that times today are tough and it is difficult to generate growth. Others might say that these four companies are simply maturing and will never be able to recapture the heady growth rates of their youth. We disagree. In fact, we argue that growth is possible in any company, at any point in the business cycle; it is a mind-set and a way of doing business, and companies that are bigger, smaller, older, or younger than these four can achieve it.

Throughout this book, we refer to the concept of growth as a business model that creates sustainable, profitable organic revenue increases over a substantial period of time. In this context, growth does not refer to short-lived spurts achieved by picking up on the latest industry trend or by stopgap cost cuts. To close that 50 percent gap, executives must strive to create a growth engine in their companies that will lead to sustainable competitive advantage, higher share prices, and a fun, innovative, and exciting workplace.

We found that many CEOs take a simplistic approach to growth. After a recent presentation to a group of senior executives in Chicago, the CEO of a US$4 billion company approached us and said, "I really liked your presentation—it has great stuff—but what I'm really looking for is the silver bullet."

Other clients say that their core business model is profitable but maturing and believe that new growth is virtually impossible to realize. The common cry among this group is, "We're stuck!" But the most frustrating cases we've encountered are those in which a company began on a strong footing by developing a suite of solid growth programs, only to curtail them when the investment funds required to implement them get squeezed.

Our response in every single case is the same: There is no silver bullet to growth, there is no panacea, and there are no shortcuts. If this is not the most popular answer, it is, without doubt, the most truthful one. Organic, sustainable growth comes only through carefully laid strategies and obsessive attention to execution. Along with this—and just as important—it requires long-term investment and patience.

A comprehensive growth model is complex, particularly when compared to other performance levers and initiatives at a CEO's disposal. How easy it is to reduce costs with a large-scale strategic sourcing project. An area is targeted, results are tangible, and the time period is defined by months, not years. How easy it is to slash both product delivery times and costs by 50 percent and increase delivery reliability up to 99 percent through a supply chain improvement initiative. These business improvement strategies have strong CEO appeal. The level of disruption or intrusion on the company is clearly defined, the time line is short, the risk is low, and the probability for success, which is easily measured by equity analysts, is high.

In this light, it becomes clear why CEOs, with such a cache of tried and true strategies to choose from, can justify postponing those longer term, decidedly less straightforward plans. But this is precisely the reason that growth initiatives are so rarely fully realized and the potential remains unexploited. Growth requires the successful integration of all the firm's activities; the entire value chain, the sales and the supplier market, strategy, and operations must all link, both for today and tomorrow. As the case studies in this book illustrate, building a growth engine in a company requires years—not months or quarters. It requires selfless behavior from senior management teams. It requires taking some risk and spending investment dollars in the anticipation of making even more in the future. The bottom line is that a good growth strategy is not easy to conceive or to implement.

Another important characteristic of growth is remarkably simple: Growth is inevitable. Regardless of the industry, at least one of your competitors is growing. Even in industries that are contracting or struggling through hard times, at least one competitor always finds a way to grow, even if it is at the expense of other competitors. Consider Southwest Airlines, which continues to prosper and gain market share while all the other major airlines in North America teeter on the edge of bankruptcy. What is Southwest's growth formula? Good, reliable customer service at a reasonable price. Sounds simple, doesn't it? In the steel industry, a notoriously tough business in which to achieve growth, Worthington Industries holds an equally impressive track record.

The inevitability of growth is also reinforced by our Endgames consolidation research, which we delve into in greater detail in Chapter 4. Companies can solidify their competitive position in a consolidating environment in one of two ways—either by being the most aggressive grower and acquirer or by simply surviving and growing while other competitors exit the business. Toyota has used this second method as the basis for its success in the global automotive industry. It has grown organically and produced the most competitive products, while its competitors have either exited the business or suffered declines in competitiveness.

MANY POPULAR GROWTH CONCEPTS AND STRATEGIES HAVE FAILED

The notion that growth strategies are difficult to develop and execute has been proven time and time again over the past 10 years. During the 1990s, many growth strategies soared to popularity, only to achieve mixed results in the end. These included economic value added (EVA) and other financial strategies, special purpose entities (SPEs) to unlock value through creative financing, and Internet-based strategies to attempt to cash in on the dot-com boom.

An EVA growth strategy, for example, helps managers take an almost surgical view of their businesses' financial performance and make strategic decisions as a result (see Appendix). This tool can work wonders in rising stock markets, but it often leads to strategies that are detrimental to long-term growth. The shareholders of companies that actively embraced EVA—including

Coca-Cola, Eli Lilly, and Hershey's—know all too well the damage it can inflict on share price.

No single business metric can be a panacea, and EVA is no different. In a comparison of profitability data and EVA data taken from the Coca-Cola 2002 annual report (see Figure 1.1), several interesting points emerge. First, economic profit has a high correlation—90 percent—to the current year net income. If this is the case, CEOs who adopt EVA may have conflicting motives and may be more prone to make short-term profit enhancement decisions than proponents of EVA care to admit. Second, EVA appears to be more stable as a business metric when conditions are good, as in the period from 1992 to 1997. As business conditions became more challenging, the economic profit metric may have provided Coca-Cola's managers with a distorted image of its standing.

FIGURE 1.1 NET INCOME VERSUS ECONOMIC PROFIT FOR COCA-COLA

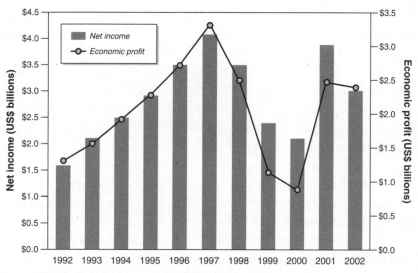

Source: The Coca-Cola Company 2002 Annual Report.

Other popular growth strategies suffer from various flaws as well. Special purpose entities and financing subsidiaries became popular as a supplementary growth engine in the 1990s, particularly in asset- and capital-intensive businesses. The idea behind these strategies is that companies could boost their growth and profits by exerting more control over their entire value chain. In turn, they could unlock value from their core business through creative financing. Again, these models worked well in a rising market, but as the economy turned south, so did the prospects of many companies that favored these strategies, including Enron, PerkinElmer, and Bombardier.

Finally, the dot-com boom created one of the most unrealistic growth mind-sets imaginable. The realities of growth seemed to vanish: Companies enjoyed boom times with endless funding and instant growth. *Seemed* is the operative word in the previous sentence. Such misconceptions about the dot-com revolution have since been laid to rest as companies continue to regain lost footing.

Internet start-ups such as the Internet Capital Group, Ariba, CMGI, and others attained market capitalization levels of tens of billions of dollars, eclipsing many of the DJIA component companies. From 1997 to early 2000, they seemed to have found a growth model that would last for decades—only to have it fall dramatically in the following months as reality set in.

The growth mantra about the convergence of media content and distribution has led to huge investments in licensing third-generation (3G) technology, especially by European telecommunications companies. Although this new technology has taken years longer than anticipated to become a reality, it is finally receiving the overwhelming consumer acceptance that was originally anticipated. Investments were financed primarily through billions of dollars of new debt, which is now being written off, causing huge losses for shareholders.

The convergence concept also led to several huge mergers in the media industry. At the time, the merger of AOL and Time Warner was expected to usher in a new era of tremendous growth and profits; today, it simply marks the pinnacle of Internet madness. The companies announced the deal based on the growth theory that AOL would control broadband Internet distribution and Time Warner would provide a content engine. As it turned out, the high valuation for AOL was unwarranted, and the Internet became flooded with content that consumers were not willing to pay for. When the business model proved unjustifiable, AOL Time Warner ended up writing off tens of billions of dollars. Disney, through its Go.com investment, and Vivendi, through its many media-related acquisitions, followed AOL Time Warner's unfortunate path in chasing the Internet growth fad. Other growth initiatives focus on changing a company's strategic business model, but carry high risk.

The moral of these stories? A growth strategy is not a plug-and-play module the senior management team can take off the shelf and use to deliver instant results to shareholders.

THE COCA-COLA CHALLENGE: GROWTH HURDLES AT THE TURN OF THE CENTURY

For a more in-depth example of how growth can present challenges to even the best of companies, look at the recent performance of Coca-Cola. As shown in Figure 1.2, Coca-Cola's revenue growth model has stalled, and its share price has declined over the past several years. Coca-Cola's revenue growth model ran out of steam in the mid-1990s, when it was hit with a confluence of issues including a succession in leadership, the Asian economic crisis, a product contamination scare in Europe, a racial discrimination suit in the United States, and a botched acquisition of the Orangina product line. In squelching the various fires, management took its eye off the company's long-term revenue growth engine to maintain its share price and higher levels of economic earnings.

The result was that Coca-Cola's senior leaders were quickly caught in the chicken-or-egg dilemma—once revenue started to fall, they began to cut selling, general, and administrative (SG&A) spending to maintain the company's high return on equity (ROE)

FIGURE 1.2   REVENUE GROWTH VERSUS SHARE PRICE FOR
             COCA-COLA

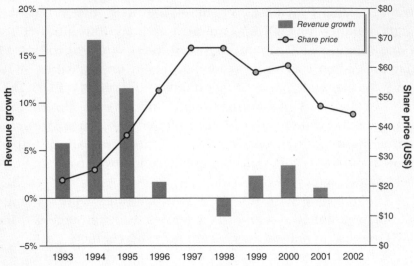

Source: The Coca-Cola Company 2002 Annual Report.

levels, EVA, and profit margins. For the first few years, the strategy
paid off. In fact, 1997 proved to be a record year for Coca-Cola's
ROE, which topped 61 percent. Also in that year, its economic
profit reached US$3,325 million, and its share price rose to US$67.
But the price for this success was steep. The same strategy that
achieved these numbers also laid the foundation for years of future
underperformance in growth and share price. By cutting the
growth lifeblood of SG&A spending, Coca-Cola went through the
latter part of the 1990s without major product launches, with
largely the same advertising messages and campaigns, and with no
new brand acquisitions or licenses with which to grow.

Since then, Coca-Cola has struggled to return to its profitable
growth-generating roots. Coca-Cola CEO Douglas Daft has continually tried to reset Wall Street's expectations for long-term
growth potential to rates of 3 percent or 4 percent. The company's
financial objectives have also shifted from revenue and profit

growth to an increase in cash flow, a metric more commonly used by mature businesses. Operationally, Coca-Cola has turned the focus of growth away from a headquarters-driven growth model and into the hands of its local market managers. This replicates the strategy of more successful growth companies such as Nestlé or Johnson & Johnson, which view local marketing execution as gritty trench warfare.

The lesson from Coca-Cola's experience is clear: A company's growth engine is difficult to build but easy to stall. Since the mid-1990s, Pepsi has gained ground versus Coca-Cola, particularly in international markets. Coca-Cola has had to reduce pricing in many markets to regain its competitiveness. Its financial performance has taken a beating, with revenue growth falling from rates of more than 7 percent to 3 percent and ROE falling from the range of 50 percent to 60 percent to current levels of 35 percent. Coca-Cola's new management team is beginning to make inroads against these challenges, but results take time to realize. In 2002, the company launched a number of popular, innovative advertising campaigns and signed several product licenses, leading to a US$2 billion growth in revenue. Coca-Cola is probably back on the growth track, but the consequences of its mid-1990s derailment have been severe.

CAN WE OVERCOME THE GROWTH CHALLENGE?

The growth challenge is greater than it initially appears. Growth that appears to be easy to realize is usually illusory or unprofitable. Tangible, formidable barriers to achieving lasting growth are in place in most companies. Chief executives are often rewarded in ways that are detrimental to building growth. Finally, many of the most popular metrics and management concepts and tools can stall growth rather than drive it.

Companies of all sizes face challenges in growing their businesses. Even companies with successful, competitively advantaged business models find their markets maturing and growth harder to come by, as underscored by Coca-Cola.

Nevertheless, growth opportunities continue to abound. There are winners and losers in every industry—why shouldn't the winner be your company? We believe that several big, global industries will consolidate rapidly over the next few years, causing immense shakeouts. The future landscape of these industries will be determined primarily on the basis of which competitors have sustainable growth engines.

In the next chapter, we elaborate on the challenges of growth. We look at the growth strategies of winners and losers in several industries and offer a perspective on how to forecast the growth prospects for your own industry.

CHAPTER 2

The Consolidation Game

Chuck Knight, the former CEO of Emerson Electric, once commented, "There's nothing like a recession to weed out weak performers in an industry." Although this assessment holds true, it is equally true that many of the headline-grabbing collapses over the past few years were self-induced.

In exploring industries that are struggling with poor growth rates, this theme of corporate Darwinism becomes crystal clear. A weak economy and uncertain business climate contribute to lagging performance, but all too often, tough economic times become the excuse and not the reason for low numbers. In case after case, we discovered that senior managers of leading companies in low-growth industries are reluctant to invest in growth-producing activities. In part, this reluctance stems from the belief that it is riskier to pursue growth strategies than to maintain the status quo. And with economic volatility running high, avoiding seemingly unnecessary risks is an attractive choice.

Let's look at a macro view of the state of growth among today's top companies. In terms of value creation, the situation is grim. The Dow Jones Industrial Average, composed of the 30 leading U.S. companies, has declined more than 5 percent in total for three consecutive years. The S&P 500 suffered a similar disappointing streak, with total declines of more than 11 percent over the same period. Indexes around the world—CAC in France, DAX in Germany, and FTSE in the United Kingdom—echoed with their own disappointing numbers.

This loss of shareholder value, in part, is the result of a confluence of factors. Geopolitical uncertainties over war and terrorism are at a boiling point, which in turn exacerbate the economic uncertainty over the duration and severity of the current downturn. Shareholder confidence also suffered a damaging blow with the spate of corporate governance scandals and ongoing questions about the integrity of audited financial statements.

Such issues continue to make growth more difficult and present companies with a host of new challenges to overcome. Still, the bottom line is that investors are not as confident about the fundamental and internally driven growth prospects of leading companies as they once were.

Driving forces of growth, such as a charismatic CEO, bold strategies, and innovation, were not limited so much by the external environment as they were by anxious, and sometimes faulty, decision making.

On the flip side, declining shareholder value is also a result of sluggish revenues. In 2001, the revenue of S&P 500 companies grew just 6 percent—including inflation. This stands in sharp contrast to steady growth rates of more than 10 percent only a few years ago.

LEARN BY EXAMPLE

Where has the growth gone? And what factors made it disappear? To find some answers, we look at the recent experience of companies in three key industries: food, pharmaceuticals, and financial institutions.

Global Food Industry

From 1975 to 1995, the consumer products industry enjoyed steady annual revenue growth rates of more than 10 percent.

Leading players capitalized on these favorable market conditions to grow quickly, and investors were rewarded handsomely.

Their secret was a winning formula for growth, which included four key points. They:

1. Invested steadily and consistently in their brands.

2. Consistently developed new products and new product categories, while constantly improving the quality and performance of these products.

3. Globalized their brands, creating vast new revenue streams in new markets, particularly in Asia.

4. Made strategic, targeted acquisitions—rarely overpaying and typically acquiring and integrating much smaller companies.

By the mid- to late-1990s, however, growth options began to dwindle. Consumers became more difficult to reach with the plethora of new media channels, with the Internet leading the pack. Most emerging markets had become fairly saturated and no longer delivered the exponential growth that consumer products companies had grown to expect. Brands battled an incredible number of new rivals for share of mind. The unsuccessful ones began to stagnate or lose their positioning.

At the same time, CEOs of these companies became victims of their own success. Their share prices had performed so well that they had to find ways to keep up the short-term growth in profitability and revenues—their shareholders demanded it, and their compensation packages frequently included heavy personal incentives for them to do it.

In short order, several events took place that prompted a huge shake-up and consolidation, radically transforming the industry. First, and most significantly, companies began to cut back on *discretionary* expenditures. But these reductions mostly included spending related to brand building and product development. In other words, as counterintuitive as it sounds, companies began eliminating the very things that made them successful in the first place.

Figure 2.1 shows actual data of one of the leading consumer products companies in the world that typified this behavior. Beginning in 1995, the company began backpedaling on its own stated principles of brand building; it throttled advertising and promotional expenses and reduced product development expenses. The reason? Senior managers sought to continue to meet the company's commitment to Wall Street to deliver superior margins and profitability.

For the first year or two, the strategy worked and earnings continued to grow, albeit at a slower pace. The stock market accepted the results, and share prices rose steadily by virtue of the prevailing bull market. However, as time passed, reality set in. Brands became less valued by consumers, who often switched to competing products, and with limited product development resources, the

FIGURE 2.1   REDUCED SPENDING IN KEY AREAS CAN AFFECT NET EARNINGS

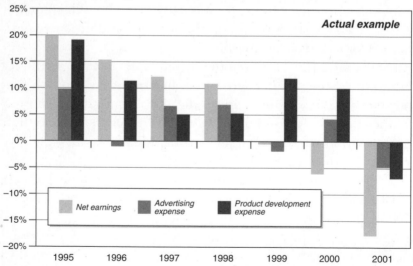

Source: Company annual reports—A.T. Kearney analysis.

company's roster of new products was sparse. By 2000, the company could no longer cover or ignore the damage that was being done. As a result, both profits and share price plummeted.

Unfortunately, this management decision-making process was copied by most of the companies in the industry. And, when combined with other factors, such as the globalization of brands, higher costs of brand building, and increased sourcing pressure from retailers, the industry experienced a tremendous shakeout through a period of rapid consolidation. Figure 2.2 shows a selection of the major players in the global food industry and their positioning on the Value-Building Growth Matrix as of December 2001. Nestlé and Unilever are the biggest players, with a number of middle-tier competitors within striking distance.

But what prompted the sudden change? Over the previous few years, a number of the industry's leading players fell two stages in

FIGURE 2.2   CONSOLIDATION IN THE GLOBAL FOOD INDUSTRY

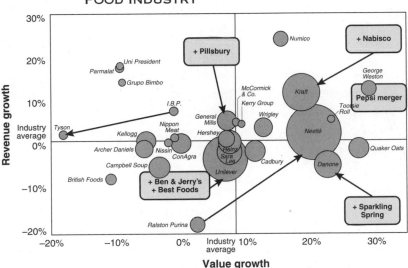

Note: Growth portfolio (CAGR 1996–2001) benchmarked against industry average. Bubble size corresponds to market capitalization.
Source: A.T. Kearney.

the Value-Building Growth Matrix: They went from the top-right quadrant to the bottom-left quadrant, and in the process they became prime acquisition candidates. The first transition, from the top-right quadrant to the bottom-right quadrant, occurred during the mid-1990s when companies began cutting back on their advertising and product development spending to maintain their margin growth. And, just as the company did in our earlier example, they were able to maintain their growth in economic earnings while their revenue growth began to curtail. The second transition, from the bottom-right quadrant to the bottom-left quadrant, happened when they ran out of margin enhancement from this cost cutting and their profitability hit the wall. As a result, their share prices fell and they became takeover candidates.

All of this activity positioned the industry for rapid consolidation, which is exactly what happened over the following 20 months. Despite the fact that mergers became somewhat less fashionable and that the media didn't cover them with the same ardor and enthusiasm as in the boom years of the late 1990s, an M&A frenzy took place nonetheless. In the process, it created a sizable gulf between the leaders and the laggards. Consider the following:

- Nestlé acquired Ralston Purina, an underperforming pet food company, made a bid for Hershey's, and is in the process of acquiring Dreyer's ice cream.

- Unilever acquired Best Foods (consumer products, particularly Hellmann's mayonnaise), Ben & Jerry's (ice cream), SlimFast (weight-management products), and Amora Maille (culinary products).

- Kraft was formed after having been spun off from Philip Morris (now Altria) and was immediately positioned as one of the three global industry leaders alongside Nestlé and Unilever. Kraft then purchased Nabisco, a leading packaged-food company.

- General Mills, attempting to keep pace as a middle-tier player, acquired Pillsbury from Diageo.

- Among the smaller players, Tyson Foods (a U.S. meat producer) acquired Iowa Beef Packers, Pepsi acquired Quaker Oats (snack foods and sports drinks), and Danone acquired Sparkling Spring (bottled water).

The result of this rapid consolidation is an industry triumvirate comprising Kraft, Nestlé, and Unilever. They not only widened the gap over their nearest rivals, but also significantly improved their profit outlook. They achieved their new power positions by following several common strategies, including:

- Raising prices as a result of their increased market share and market power.

- Increasing spending and budgets to market and brand their newly acquired products, which the previous owners were either unwilling or unable to do.

- Leveraging their greater size to increase access to product distribution channels and power.

- Increasing profit potential by wringing synergies and cost savings out of the acquired companies.

For the remaining players, the choices become a lot starker. Middle-tier players such as General Mills must seriously consider how to close the gap with the top three. For the smaller, lower performing players, it appears to be a matter of time before they top a rival's shopping list.

Pharmaceutical Industry

The same dynamics as in the global food industry also took hold in the pharmaceutical industry. Until the mid-1990s, the industry exhibited spectacular growth. Most players grew revenues and profits consistently at double-digit rates, based on the success of their R&D programs and international expansion. However, by the mid- to late-1990s, the industry began to face a number of critical challenges:

- Healthcare providers and health insurers began to consolidate their buying power to force price concessions from pharmaceutical companies.
- Important customer segments began to successfully rebel against price increases for pharmaceutical products, particularly older consumers in the United States.
- The generic drug industry reached critical mass and began successfully challenging the patent protection of a number of blockbuster drugs.
- International growth opportunities became saturated.

As a result, the management teams of many of the leading pharmaceutical companies mirrored the tactics of the consumer products company cited earlier. In this case, they began to prune research and product development budgets. The result is all too familiar to anyone who has invested in this industry. For a few years, these companies managed to maintain their growth records in profitability, but by the turn of the century, many began to hit the wall. Investors discovered that their new product pipelines had dried to a trickle or at best had two- to three-year gaps before any big new products would come to market. Suddenly, growth was at a premium.

The same migration patterns on the Value-Building Growth Matrix also took place. Players who had been in the top-right quadrant for decades began to fall down and then left, to become acquisition candidates. The strongest remaining players—Pfizer, Johnson & Johnson, and Glaxo Wellcome—began to consolidate the industry. Pfizer bought Warner Lambert and Pharmacia, Johnson & Johnson acquired Scios and Centocor, while Glaxo Wellcome bought SmithKlineBeecham to form GlaxoSmithKline. In the process, Pfizer, Johnson & Johnson, and GlaxoSmithKline have begun to pull away from the rest of the industry in terms of market share, presaging what could be a shakeout of equal magnitude to the consumer products industry restructuring we described earlier. At the same time, the share prices of former industry giants such as Bristol-Myers Squibb and Schering-Plough had fallen to such a low point that they were rumored to be the next takeover targets in the industry.

Global Financial Institutions Industry

The third industry in which growth prospects have diminished is the global banking industry. Growth in this industry had been explosive for the past 10 to 15 years, yet it now seems in the process of stagnating. How has this happened? What will the future hold as a result?

One of the biggest reasons for growth is that the industry has gradually been deregulated over the past 15 years. This deregulation has led to consolidation becoming the single most important growth driver for banks because it provides many key facets of a bank's growth platform and levers:

- *Scale:* Banking is a scale business, and growth by acquisition is usually the fastest way for a bank to increase scale and lower its cost position versus its competitors.

- *New customer acquisition:* One of the most difficult tasks in banking is to get customers to switch banks. Acquisitions immediately add to the new customer list. The "buying" of customers may be the cheapest way to sign up new business.

- *Geographic expansion:* Moving into new geographies on a grass-roots basis is also nearly impossible for a bank because of high start-up costs and inertia that keep customers from switching banks. As a result, growth through geographic expansion is also easiest through acquisition. This strategy also creates possibilities for plug-and-play brand leveraging into the new markets.

- *Technology:* Most of the scale economies in banking result from merging various IT systems. In addition, once merged, banks can often offer the newly acquired customers greater service features and functionality through technology as well.

All of these factors show why banks have used mergers as their primary growth tool in their domestic markets in recent years. Let's look at some examples.

In the United States, the industry has consolidated rapidly, particularly once acquisitions across state boundaries were permitted in the early 1990s. J.P. Morgan Chase and Bank of America, the current number two and three players in the United States, were both formed through a rash of mergers and acquisitions. Looking at the broader range of financial services businesses, two other U.S.-based giants, Citigroup and GE Capital, resulted from numerous acquisitions. This consolidation allowed banks to accelerate growth by creating nationwide banking networks, offering new services to customers, and offering more competitive pricing by virtue of streamlined back offices.

Deregulation has also resulted in consolidation in other countries. The famous "Big Bang" resulted in a relatively rapid consolidation of U.K. banks from the mid-1980s through the mid-1990s, with HSBC, the Royal Bank of Scotland, and Barclay's emerging as the winners. In Australia, the same sort of consolidation occurred, resulting in only four major banks today.

With the emergence of the European Union and the advent of the euro, European governments have opened the doors to consolidation as well. In 2002, France saw several megamergers culminating with the Credit Agricole-Crédit Lyonnais merger. In Germany, the government has encouraged the privatization and consolidation of the Landesbanks—the government-run rural state banks. This consolidation is expected to progress very quickly, and already several important deals have been announced.

In Japan, similar trends have emerged but sometimes for different reasons. The Japanese government has mandated a number of large mergers in an attempt to address the significant nonperforming loan problems in the Japanese banking system. In addition, the government has permitted and sometimes encouraged foreign financial institutions such as Merrill Lynch, Goldman Sachs, and GE Capital to acquire or take significant stakes in Japanese financial institutions.

In Singapore, the government has played a part in restructuring the banking industry by encouraging the consolidation of the industry from six banks as recently as 1996 to only three banks—DBS, OCBC, and United Overseas Bank—today. Moreover, DBS has moved aggressively across Southeast Asia, buying leasing companies, brokerages, and other financial institutions in Thailand and Hong Kong.

All of this merger activity has created significant growth for the winners of the consolidation race along several dimensions:

- Increased number of geographic markets to sell services to.
- Increased range of service offerings.
- Improved cost competitiveness (resulting from greater economies of scale) and ability to offer consumers more for less.
- Creation of financial services supermarkets, although this has proven to be less successful, in most instances, than originally anticipated.
- Increased range of distribution channels, through innovative partnering approaches (e.g., with supermarkets or online brokers).

Where does the industry stand today, and what are the growth prospects for its future? An examination of the Value-Building Growth Matrix for the industry shows a mixed bag of results. All told, financial performance has declined, shifting players from right to left on the matrix. This is largely a result of poor lending practices in the late 1990s because of unrealistic expectations of the Internet boom, especially toward telecommunications companies and 3G technology players. The industry is also showing aftereffects of its acquisitions binge in the late 1990s, particularly among U.S. firms. The financial and revenue performance of the largest players—HSBC, Citigroup, J.P. Morgan Chase, and Bank of America—has caused them to migrate toward the middle of the chart. Certainly HSBC and Citigroup had been nearer to the value-grower quadrant for many years before (see Figure 2.3).

Most banks these days are almost dormant in terms of growth as they clean up their balance sheets and repair their reputations after a number of insider trading scandals and other improprieties. Only HSBC has made a few modest moves to grow, expanding in China and India and acquiring Household International in the United States.

As we look to the future growth strategies in the industry, we see several trends emerging, all of which point to an acceleration of M&A activity, both in terms of the number and of deals.

First, although the banking industry is enormous and some of the leaders in the industry are huge, the banking industry is one

FIGURE 2.3   CONSOLIDATION IN THE GLOBAL FINANCIAL SERVICES INDUSTRY

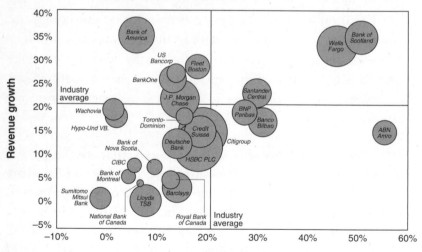

Note: Growth portfolio (CAGR 1996–2001) benchmarked against industry average. Bubble size corresponds to market capitalization.
Source: A.T. Kearney.

of the least consolidated industries in the world. As we can see from the Endgames Curve shown in Figure I.3 in the Introduction, the sum of the market shares of the top three global competitors is only 11 percent, and the Hirschmann-Herfindahl index value is similarly low. The Endgames model strongly suggests that the banking industry is about to experience a flurry of consolidation activity.

Second, a number of governments that have been notorious in dragging their feet on deregulation seem ready to capitulate. The Indian government, long opposed to allowing majority foreign ownership of its banks, opened the door for foreign banks in its February 2003 budget. Both Italy and Spain are beginning to consider deregulation and a lifting of foreign ownership restrictions. And in Canada, where the government has long resisted bank consolidation or foreign takeovers, the mood among politicians seems to be shifting toward consolidation.

The Canadian case is particularly interesting. Canadian government officials considering the question of bank mergers view the current Canadian banking landscape as healthy, dynamic, and cost-competitive for consumers. They worry that prices for banking services would increase if consolidation took place. But the reality is quite the opposite. When we look at Figure 2.3 again, we see that Canadian banks are significantly underperforming the global leaders. By allowing consolidation and foreign competition to buy their way into the market, economies of scale would occur and prices to consumers would fall dramatically. Another concern—guarantees on the provision of banking services to customers in remote areas—could easily be legislated or provided for during the merger negotiation process. In short, the argument against allowing consolidation doesn't hold water, and consumers, as well as the industry as a whole, would benefit greatly from a consolidation wave.

The third trend that will drive the next consolidation wave is cross-border synergies. Few companies have pulled this growth lever, but almost every player seems to be eyeing it with interest. Only two truly global banks exist today: Citigroup and HSBC. But the next tier of competitors aspires to that position, and those competitors are aggressively positioning themselves to attain it. Their path has already been demonstrated by leading competitors in several other industries adjacent to banking: GE Capital in leasing, Goldman Sachs in investment banking, and Merrill Lynch in brokerage. Who will strive to become the next global leader? Crédit Lyonnais? The Royal Bank of Scotland? Westpac from Australia? The Royal Bank of Canada? The Development Bank of Singapore? The race appears to be on!

What will the future landscape of the banking industry look like? A couple of points are certain. No player is assured of a leadership position, and because of the fragmented nature of the global industry, any player has a shot at reaching the top. Also, any competitor wanting to ensure growth must have an aggressive acquisition plan in place and become expert at integrating acquisitions quickly and effectively. Finally, while industry observers are sometimes overwhelmed by the size of today's industry leaders, we could easily see several banks with trillions of dollars of assets lead the industry in just five years or so. The size of the global leaders like Citigroup today may be considered small in comparison.

Beyond these predictions of market share and size, other factors may collide, potentially creating even more growth opportunities for banks and financial institutions. First, consider the insurance industry. Almost as fragmented and unconsolidated as the banking industry, the insurance industry faces significant challenges that will almost certainly include a rash of mergers. However, banks and insurance companies may also be tempted to merge with each other. This would offer growth opportunities by creating new products that combine savings and insurance product attributes, as well as the potential to sell directly to each other's customers.

Also, throughout the 1990s, many banks pursued acquisition strategies in related businesses to build *financial services supermarkets*. Among others, J.P. Morgan Chase, Credit Suisse, and Deutsche Bank diversified into investment banking, GE Capital into funds management and consumer credit, and Citigroup into investment banking and insurance. But in recent years, the benefits of this diversification have not been realized. The investment banking business has been hit by a wave of investor backlash from accounting scandals, insider trading, and analyst misrepresentation. This has sullied the reputations of many of the banks that own the investment banking businesses and turned into a significant distraction for senior management. In addition, the financial services supermarket concept does not appear to have generated the boost in shareholder value that once seemed likely. Pruning costs and selling the same services to new customers is a relatively easy postmerger integration step. But cross-selling insurance to a brokerage customer or credit cards to a leasing customer is much more difficult. As a result, it also seems likely that some of the financial conglomerates will break up into their respective pieces and return to their roots.

What do these three industry analyses tell us about the state of growth today? Growth is harder to come by in tougher times. In addition, management actions and decisions of the past have a profound impact on today's growth prospects, and a huge harvesting of growth opportunities was taken throughout the late 1990s. Finally, the issues of growth and industry consolidation intertwined. On the one hand, when growth prospects in an industry diminish, it can trigger a round of rapid industry consolidation. On the other hand, government deregulation and support of privatization can lead to companies generating growth largely through executing M&A and industry consolidation strategies. In any case, the strongest players in any industry will be able to capitalize and prosper both through organic growth strategies and through M&A-driven strategies.

Several generalizations can be made about growth strategies for individual companies:

- Sustaining growth is a complex and long-term process.
- Growth in any industry is usually governed by the successful execution of only a small number of fundamental growth drivers.

- Growth cannot be sacrificed or compromised by short-term—or Wall Street's—demands or expectations; growth is a long, uninterruptible journey.

- Companies that fail to grow or have interruptions in their growth trajectory will be acquired by the industry leaders.

- On the other hand, industry leaders have the flexibility to tailor their growth strategy to take advantage of short-term opportunities or to acquire weaker players when their valuations become attractive.

In general, the most successful companies in an industry are those that have strong, enduring organic growth prospects and strategies but that also use acquisitions as one of many growth tools, typically buying smaller competitors with strong complementary capabilities. These companies also generally have a great deal of expertise in integrating acquisitions.

Having examined the growth prospects and situation in individual industries, we now raise our sights and consider the role and performance of government in creating and fostering growth.

CHAPTER 3

Governments Can Help and Hinder Growth

Much of our discussion of growth so far has centered on the constant theme that companies create their own destiny. Even during an industry's darkest hours, there is always a company that is able to shine and outgrow its competitors. Being able to ride out market downturns, as well as take advantage of its upswings, is one of the key benefits of the growth engine. Still, no company stands alone, and as globalization continues to play an increasingly larger role in a company's corporate strategies, the shape of the global stage will have a profound impact on the growth companies are able to achieve.

After the events of September 11, 2001, many analysts speculated that the pace of global integration would slow significantly. Global economic integration did suffer a significant setback, with world trade and global capital flows in decline. For the antiglobalization movement, ever present at any gathering of economic giants, September 11 vindicated its view that global integration had widened the gap between the haves and have-nots. Furthermore, the antiglobalists say that global integration has created resentments that will continue to explode into examples of international terrorism—and threats of more.

For other organizations, the message was not less global integration, but more. U.S. Federal Reserve Chairman Alan Greenspan, for instance, said in a speech at the Institute for International Economics in October 2001: "Globalization is an endeavor that can spread worldwide the values of freedom and civil contact—the antithesis of terrorism."

But globalization involves more than just the ebb and flow of economic cycles. A.T. Kearney's 2003 Globalization Index revealed that other aspects of globalization sustained their forward momentum. Political engagement has deepened, and levels of global personal contact and technological integration have continued to grow.

Companies have become acutely aware of the potential risks posed by today's turbulent world. Ironically, the great strides in efficiency made by many companies over the past decade have resulted in vulnerable supply chains. Companies have reduced inventory, outsourced noncore activities (some to offshore locations), reduced the number of suppliers, and created leaner operations. The shift to just-in-time scheduling in the U.S. automotive industry alone, for example, has saved companies more than US$1 billion per year in inventory carrying costs. But although supply chains are more efficient and costs are down, risks are up.

Many companies have made progress in identifying threats and improving security. They are balancing the tradeoffs between growth and reduced costs and the vulnerable links in their supply chain.

Many governments, for example, create positive environments for corporate growth through a variety of strategies such as removing trade and tariff barriers, deregulating industries, allowing foreign investment in national industries, and promoting target industries. Governments can also hinder growth by imposing protectionist legislation, high taxes, and other restrictions on industry.

Although the past few decades have increased openness and transparency across borders, the ongoing process of globalization is by no means a certainty. A government can effectively disrupt the cross-border activities not only for its domestic businesses, but also for foreign companies, with a few heavy-handed pieces of legislation. Similarly, the interconnected nature of supply chains means that the effect of a single event has the potential to ripple around the world.

Over the next few years and decades, governments and their constituents must decide again and again whether to push the forces of globalization ahead, stall them, or attempt to revert to impenetrable borders. In this chapter, we look at several governments and how their policies have affected growth patterns for specific industries and their companies. Using this as a foundation, we take a step further to draw some conclusions about how companies and governments might best interact and behave toward one another to foster and create growth.

INDUSTRY GROWTH RATES VARY BY COUNTRY

Although the Value-Building Growth Matrix and the Endgames Curve are most often used to assess the relative position of companies, they are just as useful in determining the relationship between countries. The measures of Value-Building Growth, calculated and positioned based on the growth performance of each country's listed companies, can vary dramatically—and prompt some interesting questions. How do countries become winners or losers in the global economy? How does the maturity of a country's economy affect its position on the Value-Building Growth Matrix? How stable is a country's position on the matrix?

In Europe, for example, Finland, Portugal, Switzerland, and Italy all experienced revenue growth of more than 4 percent per year between 1997 and 2001 (see Figure 3.1). On the other hand, Germany's revenue growth was only 1.7 percent. Why? The answer can be found by analyzing the industry structure using the Endgames Curve.

FIGURE 3.1   COUNTRIES DIFFER SUBSTANTIALLY IN GROWTH

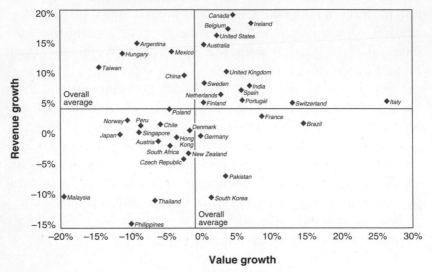

Note: Growth portfolio (CAGR 1997–2001) benchmarked against industry average.
Source: A.T. Kearney.

More and more, global capital markets punish low-growth companies with low stock price valuation, making them prime takeover candidates. The realization that sluggish growth creates companies that are relatively weaker in the global marketplace might gradually prompt policy changes in countries such as Japan and Germany, but in the meantime, other countries will continue to reap the benefits from companies that are growing both in size and stock price.

Industry structure may develop organically within a nation, based on the actions of key corporate players, or it may be fostered through targeted industrial policies.

In smaller national economies, the economic actions and results of a single corporation can often have a dramatic impact on the entire national economy and its industry structure. An example of a success story that has carried a nation is that of Nokia. In 2000, Nokia alone accounted for 68 percent of the Helsinki Stock

Exchange General Index. Its success has positively affected the overall Finnish economy. Canada experienced the same swell during the Internet boom, when Nortel dominated the valuation of the Toronto Stock Exchange.

If the corporation's fortunes change, its impact on the national economy can be destructive. Fiat, Italy's largest private employer, has played a major role in the development of Italy's economy. In the mid-1960s, an estimated 20 percent of total investments in Italy were based on production decisions made by Fiat. These decisions not only affected suppliers, but rippled out to steel, petroleum, electrical goods, and transportation industries as well. By the mid-1980s, Fiat controlled nearly one-quarter of the stock exchange through more than 500 subsidiaries and 190 associated companies. In 2001, Fiat's turnover contributed 5.6 percent of the country's gross domestic product (GDP). Now, for the first time in Fiat's history, many suspect that it may abandon its car production unit altogether. In early 2003, Fiat began laying off more than 8,000 workers, about 20 percent of its workforce. This has many people very anxious about the state of the Italian economy—particularly in terms of its deeply structured supplier industry. In fact, the Fiat effect is estimated to have reduced the Italian GDP for 2002 by at least half a percent.

GOVERNMENTS PROMOTE SPECIFIC TARGET INDUSTRIES

Governments often target and encourage the development and competitiveness of specific industries. Figures 3.2 and 3.3 show examples of a number of industrial sectors whose growth has been fostered in specific countries. In South Korea, for example, the close relationship between the South Korean government and the *Chaebols* has allowed these enormous conglomerates to become global leaders in several industries including steel, chemicals, and electronics. The same is true of Canadian banks, the U.S. high-tech industry, and the Dutch publishing industry.

FIGURE 3.2 GOVERNMENT POLICIES INFLUENCE INDUSTRIAL GROWTH (PART A)

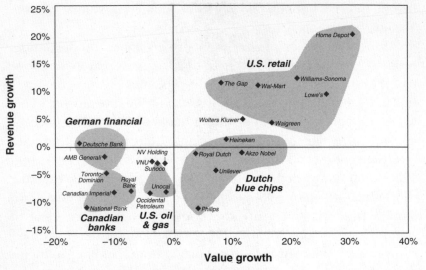

Note: Growth portfolio (CAGR 1998–2001) benchmarked against industry average.
Source: A.T. Kearney.

The effects of these national policies become particularly evident by looking at the behavior of competitors in the global marketplace. For example, the head of strategic planning of a major American chemical company told us recently, "A growth orientation would mean a total paradigm shift for us. In our company, profit is the clear first priority . . . growth is secondary." In the same vein, the head of strategic planning of a major German utility commented, "We are a zero-mistake company: Tolerating or even allowing mistakes is not part of our culture." When we remarked that without allowing mistakes, there would be no learning, and without learning, there would be no growth, the answer was, "Fair enough—then we prefer not to grow."

This view, although seemingly extreme, is in fact consistent with the general performance and valuation gap between Germany and many other Western countries.

FIGURE 3.3   GOVERNMENT POLICIES INFLUENCE
INDUSTRIAL GROWTH (PART B)

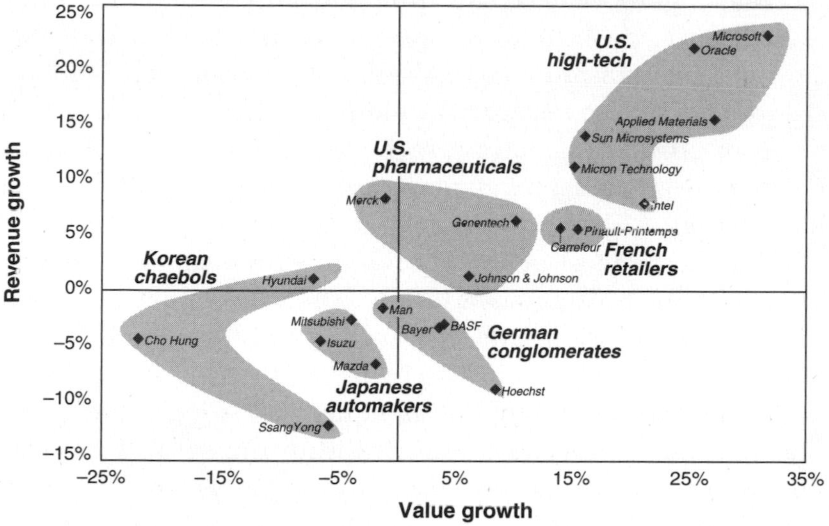

Note: Growth portfolio (CAGR 1998–2001) benchmarked against industry average.
Source: A.T. Kearney.

MIXING BUSINESS AND POLITICS ON THE ENDGAMES CURVE

What steps should governments take to nurture their corporate communities? How much corporate freedom should there be? How much legislation? What responsibilities do companies have in shaping national policies? Rather than add to the mountain of treatises on globalization, we opted to take a different tack: To gain a better understanding of the relationship between governments and corporate growth, we looked at the position of global industries along the Endgames Curve and examined corresponding government policies. This connection between the level of industry consolidation and government policy helps clarify the path to growth. The stages of the Endgames Curve are described in the following sections.

Stage 1: Opening

In Stage 1, governments have an opportunity to privatize industries, freeing them to grow in an unconstrained environment. Governments can promote innovational programs to encourage the formation of companies in industries that are in the early stages of growth. In contrast, high wages, cumbersome requirements, or overly strict regulations can inhibit growth, if not deter it altogether.

One of the most powerful tools governments can use with industries in this stage is taxation. Always a contentious topic between corporations and governments, the tax level directly affects the bottom line, which in turn directly affects a company's growth rate. In the 1980s, President Reagan's supply side tax reductions led to significant growth within the entire U.S. economy, with real economic growth averaging 3.2 percent. A number of countries, including the United Kingdom and Switzerland, found these results compelling and followed suit by lowering their own tax rates.

Two excellent examples of government-led growth promotion can be found in China and Ireland. Over the past 20 years, the People's Republic of China created six special economic zones (SEZs) designed to encourage foreign investment in China. The lure and the reward are simple: China offers foreign companies significant tax concessions to set up shop and then benefits from the new jobs, increased technical knowledge, and future tax revenues. For example, the first SEZ, Shenzhen, has played an important role in China's reform, with an annual growth rate of 31.2 percent between 1980 and 2000.

Turning to the other side of the world, Ireland's economic growth rates have been among the highest of European Union (EU) countries, with exports accounting for 96 percent of GDP. This success is largely due to the influx of offshore companies that view the Emerald Isle as an attractive location. To promote growth through investment, Ireland offers low corporate tax, a well-educated workforce, generous government incentives to overseas investors, and a commitment to open markets. It also boasts a strong history of cooperation among government, industry, and trade unions. A number of state agencies in Ireland are devoted to promoting different facets of Irish industry.

Stage 2: Scale

Stage 2 is characterized by rapid consolidation. In a domestic market, this means that the number of companies in a given industry shrinks, often at a remarkably fast pace. Because governments are generally heavily involved in Stage 1 in deregulating an industry, they tend to be more hands-off in Stage 2. Typically, the government's role in creating growth in the scale stage is limited to ensuring that the capital markets function properly and that corporate governance models work well. The presence or absence of regulations related to mergers will also affect the speed and magnitude of growth.

A good example of the government's role in Stage 2 consolidation is in the U.S. banking industry in the 1980s and 1990s. The government began to promote consolidation in the industry initially by allowing mergers across state lines. Regional banking powerhouses such as NCNB (later NationsBank) began to consolidate smaller rivals, capitalize on economies of scale, and build regional brand strength among consumers. Later, in the 1990s, the government encouraged further consolidation by repealing the Glass-Steagall Act and allowing banks to move into investment banking. This led to a number of acquisitions including First Boston by Credit Suisse and Salomon Brothers by Citigroup. The concept of a *financial services supermarket* emerged from this period of consolidation, with banks believing that they could cross-sell a number of financial services products and services to consumers, from insurance to credit to leases to savings and investment products, thus dominating consumers' share of wallet. Unfortunately, this strategy has never worked as experts expected, and many of the financial supermarkets could be unwound in the near future.

Additional examples of industries in this stage include the British banking industry and the Canadian oil and gas industry. Both of these have been consolidated over the past decade, with the consolidation characterized by a rash of mergers and acquisitions. Looking to the future, two Stage 2 industries in particular will be interesting to watch. The first is China's automotive industry, where there are currently more than 100 competitors, both foreign and domestic. This number should consolidate, both through mergers and by competitors going out of business, to a number well under 20 over the next decade. The second is the global airline industry, which is currently plagued by weak customer demand, overcapacity, and rising costs because of security, energy prices, and wage rates. Much of the overcapacity is driven by national pride of many countries insisting on having a national airline and protecting landing rights and gate access to discriminate against foreign competitors. Until the major countries of the world agree on a framework to eliminate these protectionist measures, the structure and economics of the global industry are unlikely to improve.

Stage 3: Focus

Stage 3 industries are characterized by the emergence of global leaders. Here, governments typically again exert greater influence. One of the most significant positions a government can take is to help develop and promote or protect global industry leaders. Although the United States, for example, generally promotes global free trade, it has from time to time imposed tariffs or quotas on imported products in Stage 3 industries. Most recently, these have included steel and forestry products.

In small to medium-size countries, promoting global leaders is a tall order. Consider the Netherlands and Australia. In both countries, the major banks—ABN Amro in Holland and the four major banks in Australia—face a significant dilemma. On one hand, they have consolidated their domestic industries and now their respective governments must decide whether to free them to expand aggressively overseas. On the other hand, because these companies have become so large, they are increasingly attractive to large global competitors as plug-and-play acquisition targets that would immediately provide a dominant local presence in the domestic market.

Stage 4: Balance and Alliance

By the time industries reach the fourth and final Endgames stage, they have become global leaders. They are now sufficiently concentrated so that government re-regulation, or antitrust legislation, may become an issue. A good example is the current situation in the U.S. tobacco industry, where federal and state governments are attempting to harvest the enormous amounts of cash generated by the industry in an attempt to offset the healthcare-related costs of treating illnesses caused by smoking.

The government role in the global airplane manufacturing industry is also an interesting case study. At one point many years ago, Boeing was the only major manufacturer of commercial airliners. Several European governments banded together to create a competitor, Airbus, which was a highly controversial move. Although Airbus operated with significant losses for many years and despite U.S. government claims that Airbus's losses were effectively a European government subsidy, Airbus eventually emerged as a significant player in the global airline industry.

Another interesting dynamic, particularly among Stage 4 industry leaders, is the issue of globalization and global brand prominence. Coca-Cola, Altria (formerly Philip Morris) and its flagship cigarette brand Marlboro, and Nike have created three of the world's most recognized brand names. Because of this prominence, they have also been the target of a grass-roots backlash against globalization and perceived Western dominance. Rather than re-regulation at a government level, this backlash has resulted in organized, international riots and protests at G8 meetings (an informal group of eight countries: Canada, France,

Germany, Italy, Japan, Russia, the United Kingdom, and the United States) and World Economic Forum summits.

HEIGHTENED LEVELS OF PROTECTIONISM

As previously mentioned, protectionism is a primary factor in the rate of industry consolidation. It is also one of the most potent levers a government can wield in terms of enabling or curtailing growth. Governments use protectionist measures such as import restrictions, quotas, taxes, duties and tariffs, foreign ownership restrictions, and immigration restrictions and quotas to protect or insulate a domestic industry from foreign competition. As we have seen in the preceding Endgames stage analysis, increased protectionism can stifle global competition and become a barrier to growth.

Looking to the future, there seems to be a fairly strong case to be made that governments will increasingly resort to protectionist measures in the short to medium term. It is important for business leaders seeking growth to understand these dynamics and factor them into their growth strategies. The factors behind the prediction of increased protectionism include:

- *Labor protectionism:* Globally, governments are becoming more concerned about competition in labor markets. In the United States, for example, Senator Fritz Hollings is proposing restrictions on exporting call center and customer service center jobs to India. In Europe, there is strong resistance from labor unions to opening borders to immigration. Such sentiments point to tighter restrictions on companies' ability to both hire a less expensive workforce within their own borders and deploy jobs to other countries.

- *Capital mobility:* The heightened threat from terrorism and international crime syndicates leads many experts to believe that countries will begin to limit capital repatriation and impose restrictions on foreign direct investment (FDI) and capital inflows. Already Brazil and Argentina are limiting FDI, and other countries are considering how best to control the repatriation of profits by multinational companies.

■ *Threats to globalization and global free trade:* Because of the recent political disputes between the United States and some European countries and because of the EU's refusal to consider reducing agricultural tariffs, World Trade Organization trade negotiations appear to be in jeopardy. Should the talks fail to produce freer trade, most experts believe that both the United States and the EU will increasingly focus on bilateral rather than multilateral trade agreements. A recent example of this is the U.S.-Singapore Free Trade Agreement.

The bottom line is that globalization is neither inevitable nor irreversible. Growth strategies will have to be carefully crafted and monitored to take this recent dynamic into account and navigate through barriers posed by protectionism in specific countries, markets, and industries.

A BRIEF WORLD TOUR

To further illustrate the specific roles that governments can play in setting public and industrial policies that foster growth, we consider the diverse cases of Canada, Singapore, Germany, and the United States.

Canada

In Canada, the government's record at creating growth is mixed. On one hand, the government has built a solid foundation for growth by ratifying the North American Free Trade Agreement (NAFTA). This agreement, combined with a low Canadian dollar in recent years and slightly declining tax rates, has propelled

Canadian exports to the United States to record heights. As a result, Canadian business has enjoyed almost a decade of unprecedented growth and prosperity.

On the other hand, the government has traditionally impeded growth through its privatization policies (see Figure 3.4). For example, it shields a number of Canadian industries from foreign takeovers through foreign ownership limits and restrictions, with particularly strict measures in the banking, telecommunications, and media industries.

The government has also failed to generate significant new growth by promoting innovation and nurturing new industries. This was particularly evident during the dot-com boom when many Canadian entrepreneurs migrated to the United States in a so-called brain drain. In fact, during the 1990s, Canada suffered a net loss of skilled workers to the United States in several key knowledge-based occupations. To make matters worse, Canadians

FIGURE 3.4   CANADA'S ECONOMY AND INDUSTRY POLICIES POSE CHALLENGES FOR ITS COMPANIES TO BECOME GLOBAL LEADERS

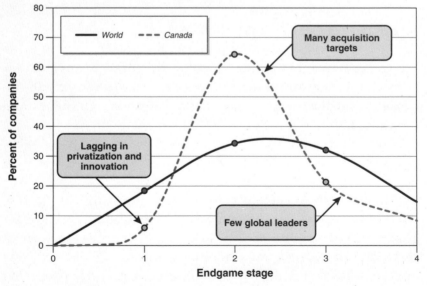

Source: A.T. Kearney.

who moved to the United States were more than twice as likely to hold a university degree than immigrants to Canada. Canadians earning more than Can$150,000 were more than seven times as likely to leave Canada as the average taxpayer.

There have been some Canadian winners in industries at later stages of consolidation. Alcan in the aluminum industry, Potash Corporation of Saskatchewan in the fertilizer industry, and Inco in the nickel industry are all Canadian companies that have emerged winners by mastering the global consolidation game. But Canada struggles with more than its fair share of unsuccessful industries. Over the past few years, many of the headlines in the nation's business sections share a common and disheartening theme:

- In the beer industry, Labatt's sold out to Interbrew.
- Seagram's sold its spirits business to Diageo and Pernod-Ricard.
- In the oil and gas industry, Canadian independent producers have been gobbled up by major global oil companies for decades.
- Canadian clothing retailers are gradually being bought out (or bankrupted) by foreign giants.

In each case, Canadian business leaders and observers wonder: Could the government be doing more to promote and encourage global leadership aspirations by Canadian companies?

Canada is not alone in its struggles to create and foster companies that can compete on a global scale. Other similar size economies such as Australia, Italy, and the Netherlands face comparable issues. In Australia, for example, the government is embarking on a privatization program in its rail, agriculture, and utilities industries. The Australian government is also considering removing its *four core banks* strategy, freeing them to grow further in both domestic and foreign markets. In Italy, the government is trying to build scale among competitors in its banking industry by encouraging consolidation and privatization.

Singapore

In Singapore, which has a relatively small economy, the government has adopted a strong hands-on approach to opening up growth opportunities for Singaporean industries. For the most part, it has done a good job. Its strategy has been to balance Singapore's industrial mix with stable, mature industries such as banking and telecommunications and newer, higher growth industries such as electronics, education, and pharmaceuticals.

To a certain degree, the Singapore government affects its industrial policy through its ownership or control over businesses through various investment vehicles, including Temasek Holdings and the Singapore Government Investment Corporation. For example, in the banking industry, the government encouraged three bank mergers over the past seven years. It also promoted the regional expansion of the nation's leading bank, the Development Bank of Singapore (which is partially owned by Temasek Holdings), by supporting mergers across Southeast Asia and Hong Kong. The government has also supported Singapore Telecommunications' (which is also partially owned by Temasek Holdings) expansion into Australia and other countries.

Singapore's industrial flexibility and growth orientation are best demonstrated by its response to recent economic and geopolitical challenges. The four traditional industrial pillars of Singapore's economy—real estate development, banking, ports and shipping, and electronics—have each suffered slowdowns recently because of the Asian economic crisis, the broader global slowdown, and the Iraqi war. In addition, the severe acute respiratory syndrome (SARS) scare virtually wiped out the tourism and convention industries from March to June 2003.

But by promoting and investing in new industries, the government is creating potential growth engines, offsetting the slower growth in its mature industries.

Education and Training

By encouraging top business schools such as INSEAD and the University of Chicago to set up satellite headquarters and teaching facilities, Singapore has become the regional leader for business education and skills training.

Pharmaceutical and Biotech

Singapore is developing leading-edge capabilities in the pharmaceutical and biotech industries by enticing leading global companies to locate their Asian headquarters in Singapore. The government is also creating research centers in Singapore and is encouraging leading scientists to move their research programs to Singapore.

Disease Management and Security

Singapore has even used its aggressive and successful response to SARS as a growth opportunity. The government's quick response helped contain the outbreak much more effectively than in other countries, particularly China and Taiwan. And it's using this victory to lure call center and data-intensive businesses away from other countries that may be deemed less safe.

Germany

Although German growth has slowed since the mid-1990s, its industrial policy continues to be a powerful weapon. The rise of Bavaria from a mainly agricultural country to a high-tech center is the result of well-targeted industrial policy. In 1994, Bavaria launched its *laptops and lederhosen* program of subsidies for high-tech companies. The result is an incredible success story that includes 120 new biotech and information technology firms opening in Munich, which is now the world's fourth-largest biotech center and boasts the second-lowest jobless rate in Germany.

The German government provides an example of industry-friendly regulation, where it, unknowingly perhaps, promoted innovation in high-speed cars through the general absence of speed limits on the autobahn. In this high-speed environment, German automakers developed cars suited to the wants of their consumers and faced only limited competition from other national car industries whose motorists faced tighter speed restrictions.

But even Germany's growth record has a few marks against it. An example of *unfriendly* industry legislation in the promotion of scale was the German purity law, which, in addition to requiring the brewing of beer from only barley malt, hops, and water, prohibited non-German brewers from entering the German market. True, this law resulted in great beer, but it also succeeded in keeping the German beer industry fragmented with small, regional players while the foreign players adjusted to global competition through consolidation. The German players are now under heavy attack from much larger foreign brewers including Interbrew, Newcastle, South African, Heineken, Carlsberg, and Anheuser Busch. It's likely only a matter of time until the last German brewery is sold to a foreign firm.

Similarly, the German telecom industry was subject to tight regulations to keep foreign firms from entering the domestic market. These regulations resulted in slow-moving German competitors with high margins that were not forced to compete through innovation. The effect was that, until a few years ago, the technology of a German telephone was seven years behind the global standard and cost twice as much.

The density of rules and regulations also plays a key role in inhibiting growth of German companies. For example, in social-democratic Europe, the state is governed by *Staatsverständnis* (state-philosophy), which is based on the principal: More freedom through more regulations. Throughout history, this overregulation has meant that founding and running a company in Europe is extremely laborious or sometimes impossible to do. For example, the craftsmen regulations *(Handwerksordnung)* are a perpetuation of a practice dating back to medieval times with the exclusive privilege of the *meisters* to open businesses.

This, along with high minimum wages, strict labor legislation that makes it difficult to lay off people, and an expansive social security program, has encouraged the rise of a black-labor market, which is roughly 17 percent of the whole economy. Because maintaining a comprehensive labor system justifies the existence of several state officials with lifetime employment, the system is, not surprisingly, difficult to change. The incarnation of this whole system is the clear overrepresentation of the labor unions in the German parliament. Labor unions account for 40 percent of seats, though representing only 16 percent of the population. Germany's high labor cost and the regulatory environment drive entrepreneurs and companies out of the country—to Poland, Ireland, North America, India, and China.

United States

In the United States, the government has adopted a position that generally supports free markets and the growth of its corporate citizens. Wage-setting mechanisms are relatively decentralized, leading to competitive labor costs, because unions have less influence over the setting of pay in the private sector than in other countries. Corporate taxes and minimum wages are also relatively low, thus promoting the existence and growth of companies in the early stages of the Endgames Curve.

The consolidation of companies in the middle of the Endgames Curve is generally supported by U.S. industrial policy. For example, the Gramm-Leach-Bliley Act was signed into law in late 1999. This repeals the 66-year-old Glass-Steagall Act and allows banks, securities firms, and insurance companies to affiliate within a new financial holding company structure.

Companies in Stage 4 of the curve are at risk of facing challenges from the U.S. government. In the past, regulation of prices and operations was used to control monopolistic industries such as transportation, power, or communication. In recent decades, the U.S. government has instead used antitrust laws in its effort to protect consumers through competition. This mostly has been undertaken by using antitrust legislation to block mergers that may create monopolies or promote monopolistic behavior. One of the best-known recent examples of U.S. antitrust action was against Microsoft. In 1998, the Department of Justice filed an antitrust complaint against Microsoft based on the belief that the company has used its market power to override the checks and balances of free market competition. The decision two years later was that Microsoft had violated antitrust laws, illegally maintaining its monopoly over computer software operating systems. On later appeal, the court threw out a previous order that would have split up the company, and Microsoft has emerged relatively unharmed.

Another example of the U.S. government's effort to inhibit mergers is the U.S. Airways-United Airlines US$12.3 billion merger plan, which collapsed in July 1991 after the Department of Justice stated it would sue to stop the deal.

A final example of the U.S. government's inhibiting a company in late stages of the Endgames Curve is in the tobacco industry. Here, the government has been involved in a rash of lawsuits, aimed at recovering some of the healthcare costs resulting from smoking and exposure to secondhand smoke. Recently, large U.S. companies including Philip Morris, R.J. Reynolds, and British-American Tobacco have been under siege, facing a multitude of lawsuits. The largest, a federal lawsuit first filed in 1999, seeks compensation for US$289 billion and asserts that the major cigarette corporations have manipulated nicotine levels and lied to consumers. Another suit, settled in early 2003, ordered Philip Morris to pay US$10.1 billion in damages to consumers and the Illinois government for misleading smokers into thinking that "light" cigarettes were safer than other varieties. Facing growing restrictions at home, tobacco companies are shifting focus to marketing their products in developing countries.

LESSONS LEARNED

In this chapter, we have seen several examples of how governments intervene to promote or hinder growth. Depending on where your company's operations are focused, governments can help your growth strategy, impede it, or not affect it at all. Regardless, it is important for companies to recognize how governments impact their growth prospects and their competitive position. In addition, it does sometimes make sense for companies to lobby governments on specific growth-enabling issues to achieve a level competitive playing field or even to gain an advantage (in this respect, playing catch-up through lobbying efforts is always more difficult than being proactive—just ask executives at Kodak or in the U.S. automotive or steel industries). We encourage you to examine governments' impact on your growth prospects from both a macro- and microstandpoint and develop a component of your growth strategy around government-specific issues and opportunities.

This concludes the first part of the book. We now turn our focus from illuminating the issues and barriers to growth to looking at the financial and economic rationale to pursue growth.

PART II

THE CASE FOR GROWTH

CHAPTER 4

The Growth Objective

Why should a company grow? The short answer: If a company is not growing, it cannot be successful over the long term. Add it to death and taxes as one of life's certainties.

We know this, without doubt, through both our research and experience. We analyzed and correlated hundreds of variables to identify the best predictors and drivers of business success. Long-term, profitable revenue growth, as it turns out, accounts for 78 percent of a company's share price performance over a 14-year or greater period of time. This stands in stark contrast to more static measures of a company's performance such as net income, return on sales, return on equity, or return on invested capital, which account for only 22 percent. Long-term revenue growth is the most important corporate strategic objective for any company that aspires to healthy performance in the stock market.

The corollary to the growth imperative is the long-term impact of industry consolidation. As we discussed in the Introduction, companies must win the consolidation battle in their industry or face the stark prospects of being acquired or going out of business. So the growth imperative becomes doubly important in terms of your company's survival. Either your company grows and becomes more successful, or it faces poor financial returns, acquisition by a stronger competitor, or extinction. It truly is a survival of the fittest scenario.

The good news is that the benefits of profitable growth are huge. The analytical framework we use as a road map to improved competitiveness is the Value-Building Growth (VBG) Matrix. As we've mentioned, the VBG Matrix is a tool that A.T. Kearney has developed and honed over the past 14 years. Based on a database of the financial data of 29,000 companies from around the world, the VBG framework offers credible information and insight about the competitive landscape and strategic options for virtually every industry.

The case for steering your company into the top-right corner— the value-growing quadrant—is compelling. As shown in Figure 4.1, value growers have enjoyed extremely strong business performance over the past 14 years: a compound annual growth rate in revenues of 18 percent and a compound annual growth rate in

FIGURE 4.1   A.T. KEARNEY VALUE-BUILDING GROWTH MATRIX (1998–2002)

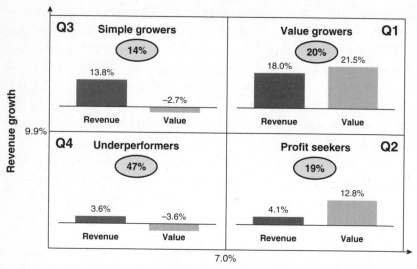

x% = Percentage of companies in quadrant.
Source: A.T. Kearney.

shareholder value creation of 21 percent. Imagine that your company achieved these results over the next 15 years.

Companies in the other three quadrants excel in either only one dimension—revenue or shareholder value growth—or none at all. The objective, then, for any company is to move from its current position to the top-right corner of the VBG matrix and then fight to stay there. In this chapter, we describe the steps companies must take to become value growers; in the rest of the book, we offer lessons on how to keep that title for as long as possible.

The first step is to create a tailored VBG chart. Companies can plot the position of most of their competitors with a relatively high degree of accuracy by using publicly available information and common spreadsheet applications. Annual reports and SEC documents pinpoint the location on the vertical axis, while historical share price determines the position on the horizontal axis. We find it is most helpful to plot each company's data point on a bubble plot, using current-year revenues to determine the size of the bubble.

With a customized matrix in hand, executives can take stock of their company's relative competitive position within their industry. Whatever the starting point, the destination is always the same: the top-right value-growing quadrant. Consequently, the next step is to chart a course toward this goal, toward becoming an industry leader. Regardless of how big or how small an industry is, it is the largest, most profitable competitors that have the most strategic levers to control their own destinies: They have the size to dictate how competition will evolve within the industry, they have the muscle to squeeze weaker competitors, they have the resources to aggressively pursue new growth opportunities, and they have *acquisition currency* in the form of an above-average share price.

FIND THE RIGHT PATH

Regardless of a company's starting point, the journey to the value-growing quadrant takes time, often several years, but it's a necessary trip. In our experience, an explicit strategy to remain in one quadrant, *other than the value-grower quadrant,* is rarely successful. With this in mind, we look more closely at the different quadrants and the various strategies companies should consider when mapping their individual routes.

Underperformers

Companies in the lower-left corner of the VBG matrix are the underperformers of their industry. Having fallen on hard times, their businesses are not expanding, and they have become the pariahs of the financial markets. If they do not improve their competitive standing, they risk being acquired by a larger, more successful player—or they go out of business. The only escape route is to adopt a comprehensive turnaround and restructuring program.

The odds are not encouraging. Only a handful of companies have successfully turned themselves around from being an industry underperformer to a value grower. But it can be done. Despite IBM's recent lethargy in terms of revenue growth, its turnaround under the leadership of former CEO Lou Gerstner was remarkable. When Gerstner took the helm at IBM in 1993, the company was primarily a computer hardware manufacturer. It focused on mainframe computers, which were becoming a commodity product; and although it competed in the PC market, it was a high-cost producer. The bad news continued: Its balance sheet was debt-laden, its growth prospects were poor, and its share price was hitting all-time lows.

Undaunted, Gerstner developed and executed a strategy along both the revenue and value dimensions of the VBG matrix. On the revenue side, he recognized that the strongest future growth prospects for IBM lay not in the brutally competitive area of hardware, but in software and services. Over the next decade, Gerstner built IBM Global Services from nothing to become the world's largest management and solutions consulting firm. The unit quickly became a powerful growth engine and now accounts for about 45 percent of Big Blue's revenue. Gerstner capped off the expansion into consulting services by acquiring Pricewaterhouse-Coopers in late 2002. Gerstner also pursued growth in the software industry with the same level of aggressiveness, but relied more heavily on acquisitions than on internal growth, to get the ball rolling.

On the value side, Gerstner focused on reducing costs and improving the balance sheet by repaying debt. Historically, IBM resisted massive layoffs, but, as an outsider, Gerstner was able to significantly reduce administrative costs and headcount, improving IBM's competitiveness. Later, Gerstner expanded this strategy by shifting IBM's resource base from higher cost Western countries to lower cost emerging countries including India and China. Most industry observers believe that this offshore strategy alone gives IBM a 1 percent to 2 percent cost advantage over its competitors.

Gerstner's turnaround program was both bold and risky and required nearly a decade to fully implement. But the effort and gamble paid off: Today, IBM's strategy stands out as a great model for companies seeking to reverse their fortunes.

Companies that are unable to break out of the underperforming quadrant quickly enough, however, may soon become the target of a value-growing competitor's acquisition strategy. In the financial services industry, GE Capital has built its business—and achieved value-grower status—by acquiring smaller, underperforming rivals. Its strategy, in fact, is strikingly simple. As one of the largest competitors in the industry's value-grower quadrant, it buys fundamentally strong companies in the underperforming quadrant of the VBG matrix and fully integrates them into its core business.

For example, when Eastern European economies suffered a downturn in the mid-1990s, GE Capital went on a buying spree, acquiring those competitors that had the strongest business prospects but were suffering through temporary liquidity crunches. General Electric followed the same strategy in Thailand and South Korea following the Asian economic crisis in 1997 and in Japan in the late 1990s after the Japanese government opened its doors to foreign investors in the financial services industry.

GE Capital is able to finance such acquisitions cheaply for two reasons: It generally boasts a strong stock price, and it buys when valuations are low. It is also able to immediately implement a lower capital cost structure into its acquisitions by virtue of the triple-A credit rating of its parent company, General Electric.

In terms of integrating its acquisitions, GE Capital wastes little time. Typically, within 60 days of closing a deal, GE Capital installs its own management team, rebrands the acquired company under the GE Capital logo, and fully establishes its own management processes and financial controls. A good example of this integration process in action is GE Capital's purchase of a package of nonperforming consumer loans from the Thai government following the Asian crisis in 1997 and 1998. GE Capital built a 300-member collection team from the ground up—something that had never been done before in Thailand. Team members traveled the Thai countryside by car and motorcycle collecting loans and reminding customers to pay off their outstanding balances. The strategy allowed GE Capital to make a handsome return on its investment.

Current Underperformers

In the wake of the recent economic downturn, there is no shortage of restructuring candidates. Even companies that seemed untouchable just a few years ago are suddenly subject to massive overhauls. McDonald's, for example, epitomized a multinational growth company for decades; today, the fast-food giant is struggling under the weight of a number of challenges. Topping the list is meeting customers' changing needs. Consumers are not only more wary of high-fat, high-calorie foods, but also increasingly concerned about food safety following outbreaks of mad cow disease (or bovine spongiform encephalopathy [BSE]) and a spate of warnings about tainted meat and recalls. In terms of demographics, its customer base is aging, and it has not been able to hold onto its younger target base.

Second, the quality of McDonald's store operations has deteriorated. The company experienced declining same-store sales in 2002 on the heels of flat same-store sales for several consecutive years. Customer service levels have fallen and are spotty at best, with many markets suffering from wide discrepancies in service among individual restaurants. McDonald's innovation record is also in a rut; its last hit product, Chicken McNuggets, was introduced in 1983.

Combined, these challenges have knocked the wind out of McDonald's sails. Its customer base has shrunk, and it has lost market share to traditional fast-food restaurants as well as newer format family restaurants. Furthermore, its share price has fallen from a high of US$48 in 1999 to less than $13 in 2003.

Recognizing the need for dramatic improvement, the company began at the top by bringing in a new CEO, Jim Cantalupo, in 2003. Within a few months, Cantalupo unveiled his turnaround strategy: cut capital spending by one-third; open fewer restaurants; and make basic improvements in restaurant operations, focusing on cleanliness, food and menu quality, and staff productivity. Time will tell whether this plan is successful, but the fact that it is a defensive plan, rather than an offensive one, does not bode well for its chances of producing breakthrough growth.

In devising a restructuring initiative, one of the most important questions to answer is: What is the best way to get out of the underperforming quadrant? Through the simple-grower quadrant? Through the profit-seeker quadrant? Or by growing both revenues and shareholder value simultaneously?

We discussed the possibilities with a CEO of a manufacturing company in Sweden. When he took over the leadership of the company several years ago, the company was clearly a restructuring candidate: stagnating revenues, inferior market share, and consistent losses. He restructured the business in a fairly traditional way: bare-bones cost cutting and shrinking the size of the company with the single-minded focus on increasing profits. It took four years, but he reached his goal. The next step was to begin growing again. But he soon discovered that the company's management had effectively forgotten how to grow. The restructuring rules—avoid risk, avoid mistakes, reduce costs at any cost—had become so deeply entrenched in the culture that, once given the go-ahead to grow, employees didn't know how to behave. Looking back, the CEO recognized the problem: "It's like horses: When they have plowed for several years, they can't jump anymore."

It was a costly lesson, but the CEO learned through experience that the best path to the value-growing quadrant is a direct path, with equal focus on restructuring, margin enhancement, and revenue growth (see Figure 4.2). Our research underscores this. For underperforming companies that reached the value-growing quadrant, 63 percent reached it in three years by taking a direct route. The remaining companies took an average of six years to reach their destinations, following stopovers in the

FIGURE 4.2   IN THE LONG TERM, REVENUE AND VALUE GROWTH MUST ALIGN

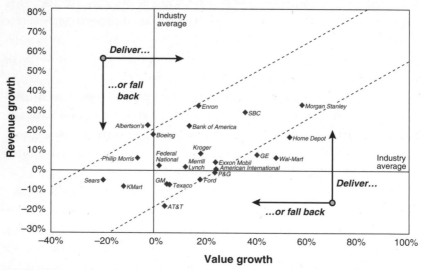

Note: Growth portfolio (CAGR 1995–1999) for U.S. companies benchmarked against industry average.
Source: Value-Building Growth Database—A.T. Kearney analysis.

simple-grower quadrant (16 percent) or in the profit-seeker corner (21 percent).

For underperformers, there is no time to waste in embarking on a restructuring program. One of the first steps is to score a quick win. Find at least one area where the company is able to expand quickly to regain some of the firm's lost fighting spirit. It doesn't have to be the most broad-reaching initiative, but it must have strong support from senior leaders and set the tone for change.

In the longer term, a restructuring strategy should be based primarily on two key planks: vision and customer focus. A strong, CEO-driven vision is important to getting back into the game by reestablishing the company's reputation as an accepted and well-respected player. The vision statement should be a simple, yet decisive, demarcation point between the old and the new directions. For example, when Ferdinand Piech, the former CEO of Volkswagen, was asked how he was going to imitate the seemingly unbeatable Japanese competitors, he shot back, "We don't imitate, we compete!" Piech thus summed up the aspirations of Volkswagen in one simple, straightforward, and powerful sentence. In the years since, Volkswagen's restructuring strategy resonated with Piech's vision every step of the way. He reengineered Volkswagen's procurement processes to reduce costs, and he simplified and standardized its vehicle platforms to reap the benefits of economies of scale. As Volkswagen regained its financial power, Piech expanded the Audi and SEAT product lines; acquired SKODA, Bentley, Bugatti, and Lamborghini; and launched the Phaeton model alongside VW's existing (and popular) Audi-A8 model to compete with Mercedes-Benz and BMW in the high-end luxury car segments. Today, Volkswagen is among the top five automakers in the world.

When a company faces a restructuring challenge, much of its attention turns inward, leaving the customer in the dark. For a company in a precarious position, this could be the fatal blow. In fact, turning the spotlight back onto the customer—and keeping it there—is critical. Ultimately, restoring customer confidence is the only way to reverse a downward trend. In looking for a good example of this, we can't help but look again at how IBM restructured in the mid-1990s. Lou Gerstner anticipated customers moving away from computer hardware and into software, solutions, and business consulting; this foresight and the strategies that evolved from it saved the company.

Simple Growers

Companies in the top-left quadrant—the simple growers—are generally able to create growth models in their business. The problem is that these growth models produce revenue growth that is not profitable; hence revenue growth does not translate into increased profitability and higher share prices. The first step that a CEO must take in this quadrant is to improve margins.

A successful margin enhancement usually takes one of two directions: outright cost reduction to achieve a lower competitive cost position and greater economies of scale or higher aggregate pricing levels that lead to improved price realization and higher margins.

In the steel industry, Nucor implemented a brilliant strategy that in effect moved it out of the pack of simple growers into the leading position in the industry. By using recycled steel as raw material and by innovating the steel rolling process, Nucor was able to lower its cost per ton to about 50 percent less than its traditional competitors. It was able to capture dominant market positions in the infrastructure, construction, home building, and automotive markets and make significantly higher margins than other competitors. Its share price skyrocketed through the late 1980s and early 1990s and, in so doing, Nucor gained a preeminent market position while forcing many competitors with higher cost technology into bankruptcy.

General Electric is also a master at executing this type of strategy in its more mature lines of business. It was a pioneer in bundling service and maintenance contracts (and sometimes leasing and financing services) with its original equipment manufacturing businesses. Through bundling, General Electric was able to increase its prices and margins and turn unprofitable stand-alone equipment businesses such as CAT scanners, locomotives, and turbines into profitable businesses.

On the other hand, many competitors in the simple-grower quadrant find themselves here because they have made the mistake of pursuing growth for growth's sake. The growth they have created does not generate a profit, and if the trend continues, these companies fall downward into the underperformer quadrant.

Let's look at some examples of companies that face this challenge.

In many parts of Asia, large industrial conglomerates dominate the national competitive landscape. In Japan, South Korea, and, most recently, China, large industrial conglomerates have been a preferred route to industrial development. These conglomerates are massive and routinely enter diverse businesses without so much as a business plan. They are sometimes protected from competition by their governments. These companies grow revenues successfully when times are good. When times are bad, it is another story. In Japan, for example, many of the big holding companies have been restructured and have divested businesses in the past few years because of Japan's poor economy. In South Korea, Daewoo, Hyundai, Lucky Goldstar, and SK Group were viewed as global powerhouses in the early and mid-1990s. They expanded into unrelated business to grow size and revenues, but their business models were susceptible to an economic shock. As a result, they took a pounding in the Asian crisis, and many have since divested the majority of their businesses or closed down. Looking to the future, the wild card is the emerging industrial conglomerates in China. Many are exhibiting phenomenal growth because China's economy is booming. But unless they move to more sustainable and competitive business models, their future is less ensured if China's economic growth deteriorates.

Another good example of the challenges in the simple-grower quadrant is DaimlerChrysler. DaimlerBenz bought Chrysler at the peak of the business cycle and at the peak of capacity in the automotive industry. Since then, the economy has collapsed and

DaimlerChrysler was forced to discount prices heavily just to move product. Its merger, therefore, has produced revenue growth but not profitable growth, and DaimlerChrysler remains stuck in the simple-grower quadrant.

Hewlett-Packard finds itself in a similar situation. It bought Compaq at the height of capacity in the PC industry. But HP has made several aggressive moves to expand its growth options. It has integrated Compaq more quickly and successfully than industry observers had expected. It has also moved into the higher growth and higher margin business process outsourcing industry and consolidated its position as a leading competitor with a landmark contract signing at Procter & Gamble. Although the jury is still out on HP's ultimate success, it has taken bold first steps to move out of the simple-grower quadrant.

Two management levers are particularly important for simple growers to pull if they are to take the first critical steps toward value-growing success: strategy and leadership. A simple grower must optimize its portfolio of products and services and focus on the products and market segments that can propel the company into the value-growers quadrant. This is what HP is trying to do with its move into the business process outsourcing market. Focusing a company on profitable growth also requires a shift in management discipline. Saying no to unprofitable or marginally profitable sales revenue is difficult, which is why a shift in thinking from the top levels of a company is often the most important symbolic step in the transition from being a simple grower to a value grower.

Profit Seekers

Companies in the bottom-right quadrant—profit seekers—are able to maintain high valuations in the stock market despite having weak revenue growth models. This positioning is not sustainable because the stock market expects a boost in revenue growth and market share over the medium to long term for a company to command a premium share price. Typically, there are two groups of companies in this category: The *soon-to-be's* and the *has-beens*. A soon-to-be company holds tremendous promise—perhaps it has discovered a new technology—but hasn't fully realized its potential in terms of revenue growth. On the flip side, a has-been company is just that: It has been a value-growing star that is losing its shine and tumbling to underperformer status.

Internet companies were excellent soon-to-be examples in the profit-seeker quadrant. They were perceived by the stock market as having huge revenue growth prospects and were accorded high valuations among investors. But as their business models became more exposed with time, they hit the wall. Do you remember when companies such as the Internet Capital Group, CMGI, Ariba, Commerce One, and Excite had huge market capitalizations but no profits and virtually no revenues? Today, most of these companies are either out of business or at a fraction of their former valuations.

More recently, several pharmaceutical companies have fallen out of the value-grower quadrant and into the profit-seeker quadrant because their research and development programs have dried up and their revenue growth has dwindled. In 2004, leading pharmaceutical companies hope to launch more than 60 products, 11 of which are aiming for peak year sales of more than US$1 billion. Most are relying on new products to address losses from patent expiry. For example, 55 percent of AstraZeneca's sales in 2000 will be off patent by the end of 2003. In the same time period, Schering-Plough will lose patents on 48 percent of its products, Bristol-Myers Squibb will lose 35 percent of its patents, and Eli Lilly will watch 28 percent of its products go off the radar screen.

As soon as their existing products go off patent, they face stiff and immediate competition from generic drug manufacturers, and their R&D pipelines have a void that means future growth prospects are still a long way off. As has-beens, their challenge is to fend off the generic competitors through product extensions or legal actions to preserve today's revenues, while accelerating their pipeline development to capture tomorrow's growth prospects faster.

Looking to the future, despite the weak stock market, a number of industries still have high valuation levels and may face a crossroads in the next few quarters. In many sectors of the high-tech industry, for example, several prominent players have maintained their high stock valuations while their revenue growth has actually stagnated or shrunk. Look at Oracle, Cisco, and Sun Microsystems. All three have lost business over the past two years while their share prices remain at relatively high values, ranked by a number of equity analysts. The key question is: How long can these companies stay in the profit-seeker quadrant before either reigniting their growth engines or falling into the underperformer quadrant? Oracle's hostile bid for PeopleSoft signals its first steps in reestablishing growth in its software and solutions business.

Utilities also seem poised for a profit-seeker shakeout. Valuations of utility companies have remained high throughout the recent economic downturn, primarily because of their defensive nature as an investment. But the industry is plagued with problems, from outdated infrastructure and high capital investment requirements to capacity problems in certain geographic areas. Warren Buffett, famous for his timely investments, believes that the industry is poised for new growth—evident in his recent heavy investments in a number of utilities.

Finally, a number of traditional blue chip companies are also facing the profit-seeker dilemma. Companies such as Procter & Gamble, Siemens, and General Electric continue to enjoy high stock market valuations but have few exciting growth prospects. With their markets maturing, management has resorted to cost-cutting to make the numbers, doing so for so long that their growth engines have essentially been extinguished. What will happen to these once-great companies? Will they reinvent themselves and begin growth again? Will they break themselves apart and release value by focusing on smaller, more distinct, and manageable pieces? Or will they slide into the underperformer quadrant?

Again, look at the key management levers to determine which strategies the profit seekers should consider. For profit seekers, the two most important levers are culture and leveraging core competencies. Profit seekers are known for their rigid—and ultimately self-destructive—cultures. The words from a senior executive of a German-based utility company epitomize the problem. When discussing his company's culture, the executive observed, "This is a no-mistake company. In whatever we do, we make no mistakes. If a crisis hits, we put on the brakes and reduce growth and revenues until we fix the bottom line." Yet mistakes are fertile ground for learning. Without the ability to learn from trial and error, how can a company innovate and grow? In the long run, it can't.

When it comes to culture, the best plan to induce growth may be to stir things up. Embracing risk within the corporate culture means encouraging an entrepreneurial spirit and allowing for experimentation—and mistakes. To be most effective, this cultural shift should be led by the company's senior leaders, with the CEO being its most vocal messenger and strongest supporter.

In terms of leveraging core competencies, we advise profit seekers to stick to their knitting and focus on what they do best. In the pharmaceutical industry, for example, when companies lost control over their research and development processes, they lost their innovation. The productivity of the R&D-driven growth engines declined and their new product pipelines dwindled. These companies failed to monitor where pharmaceutical research was being carried out most successfully—in universities, small research centers, biotechnology companies, and drug delivery technology companies—not in their own R&D labs. Instead of partnering with smaller, more innovative researchers or buying new drug ideas from these "suppliers," many of the large pharmaceutical companies stuck with their traditional innovation processes only to find that they had made a bad investment.

Remaining a Value Grower

The benefits of remaining in the value-grower quadrant are clear: a competitive, growing business that is recognized as a leader by the stock market. But staying in this quadrant over long periods of time is difficult and requires great managerial skill as we have seen in several of the case studies presented in earlier chapters.

Consider Kohl's, an American retailer that has consistently ranked as a leader in its industry (see Figure 4.3). Kohl's has grown by rolling out its format across the huge North American market and thus attaining superior growth rates and accordingly high stock prices. Its stature is unlike any other retail company in the world. Kohl's broke out of the traditional department store mold—as one of several flagship stores in shopping malls—and began to build stand-alone stores. It now has both stand-alone stores and mall stores. This strategy has served Kohl's well, propelling it 15 percent to 20 percent above the industry average and to a valuation between US$200 and US$350 billion.

FIGURE 4.3 KOHL'S HOLDS ON TO ITS VALUE-GROWER TITLE

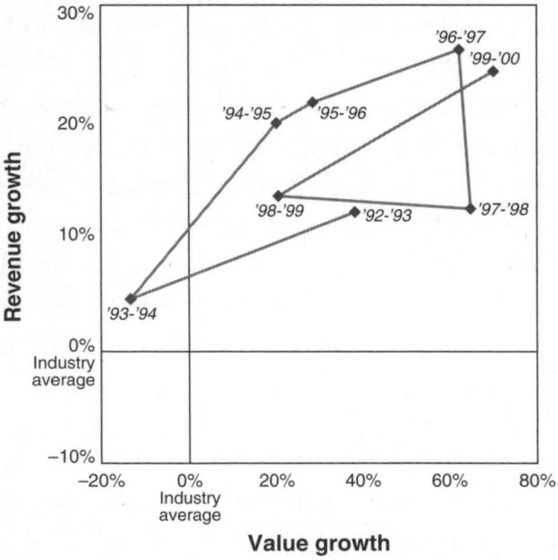

Year	Key drivers
1992	Kohl's announces its IPO
1993	Opens 11 stores
1994	Opens 18 stores
1995	Opens 22 stores
1996	Begins Midwest expansion strategy and opens 22 stores
1997	Begins national expansion strategy, acquires Bradlees Stores in New Jersey and Washington, and opens 32 stores
1998	Joins S&P index and opens 32 stores
2000	Acquires Caldor chain of 30 stores across New York and opens 60 stores

Source: A.T. Kearney.

The value-grower quadrant is the most rewarding quadrant to reach and the most challenging to remain in. Of the 29,000 companies tracked in A.T. Kearney's Value-Building Growth database, fewer than 250 companies have been able to remain in the value-growers quadrant for a long period of time (since its inception in 1988) or able to return to the quadrant after falling out for a period. The list of names is short but illustrious and includes global heavy hitters such as Nestlé, Johnson & Johnson, Wal-Mart, and Microsoft. These companies share consistent, superior performance across all key measures, making them unquestioned leaders in their respective industries. The toughest challenge is to be consistent, year after year, without a single moment of relaxation or complacency.

Looking to the future, the path forward for some value growers is as smooth as it has been in the past. Dell, for example, has been a mainstay of the value-grower quadrant. Dell's business model, supplier and supply chain management capabilities and processes, and its customer focus all position it to continue to dominate the PC industry for years to come.

But for others, some challenges may lie ahead. Microsoft has been a value grower for many years but has faced antitrust challenges in the United States and will face them in Europe as well. It also faces challenges from open architectures and Web-based applications. Microsoft is also sitting on tens of billions of dollars in cash for which it can't find attractive investment opportunities. Despite these challenges, Microsoft is pursuing several new growth opportunities, including more aggressive entry into the market for corporate services and solutions and targeting the video games and home entertainment market.

Intel, another long-time value grower, has experienced several significant challenges to its growth trajectory, and its ability to maintain its status as a value grower in the future may be in jeopardy. In the aftermath of the bursting of the Internet bubble, Intel's sales shrank dramatically, competition intensified, and its products are increasingly becoming commodities. And as the rate of technological advances slows, Moore's Law, the perpetual and exponential growth in data density, appears to be hitting a stumbling block. No one knows what the future holds for Intel, but remaining a value grower will indeed be a challenge.

PULLING ALL THE RIGHT LEVERS

We close this chapter with a brief overview of the key management levers that value-grower companies pull to remain in their leadership positions. The remainder of the book focuses on bringing these levers to life using case studies and management principles. Key management levers include:

- *Vision:* The vision of value-growing companies is always clear and consistent—to dominate their industry and establish a global leadership position. Being a competitive or well-respected industry player is not enough; there is no second best.

- *Strategy:* Value growers design their strategies to have commanding control over market share and achieve above-average growth in both the short and long term. To stay on top, value growers must constantly create new growth strategies; otherwise, they risk being overtaken by their best competitors. The lesson here is to constantly raise the bar for your competitors and take aggressive action at every turn.

- *Culture:* Complacency within the corporate culture is one of the biggest risks value growers face. Value growers such as Altria and Wal-Mart have maintained their hunger for leadership and dominance for decades.

- *Leadership:* The leaders of value-growing companies are successful at accomplishing something that very few other companies can—the concept called *walking the talk*. Leaders of these companies may debate and disagree behind closed doors, but in public they put the interests of the company ahead of everything else. In value-growing companies, leadership comes first.

- *Leveraging core competencies:* How can we do better? Do we capitalize on the best technology? Have we adopted the most effective outsourcing strategies? Do we have the lowest cost position, the shortest reaction time, and the highest quality possible? Seasoned value growers know their business deeply and understand what competencies are critical to their long-term competitive success.

- *Customer focus:* At value-growing companies, the customer always comes first. Everyday customer needs, as well as long-term customer trends, are monitored, debated, and tested daily to enable strategic decisions about how to compete and how to exceed customer expectations.

In this chapter, we took stock of a company's starting point on the voyage to growth, looking at current competitive position and the strategies that will position the company for growth. Now comes the challenge of maintaining growth over the long haul and doing so during industry consolidation. Chapter 5 reveals the secrets to long-term growth.

CHAPTER 5

Getting Ready to Grow

In the previous chapter, we showed the undeniable benefits of growth. And to help position your company to begin sustainable growth, we presented strategies for turning your company around regardless of the competitive position you are in today. In this chapter, we discuss some of the forces that companies must take into account to maintain growth over long periods of time. Keeping these in mind will help you design the best growth strategy possible and help your company stay in the value-grower quadrant.

Growth is difficult to accomplish—and even more difficult to sustain. Consider companies such as WorldCom and Enron: These were among the titans of the U.S. industrial landscape from 1995 to 1999. At the time, analysts and investors alike would have universally agreed that these companies had solved the growth riddle. How quickly times change.

So what has happened since then? Some have continued their strong performance, while others have seen their growth prospects vanish and their competitive position erode. A few snapshots illustrate the point:

- WorldCom (now MCI), the value-growing leader from 1995 to 1999, is bankrupt and has fallen from grace under massive debt, management improprieties and turnovers, and accusations of fraud and corporate misconduct. Bernie Ebbers, once heralded as a business hero, was forced to resign as WorldCom's CEO and has retreated from corporate life under a cloud of scandal.

■ Enron has endured a similar fate. Having gone through bankruptcy, Enron's former management team is being prosecuted for fraudulent conduct and accounting scandals, which also brought down its auditor, the venerable Arthur Andersen.

■ Both Morgan Stanley's and Merrill Lynch's share prices and growth prospects have plummeted because of an SEC investigation into the practices of equity analyst recommendations. A struggling economy, weak stock market, and a paucity of M&A deals have made a bad situation worse.

■ Home Depot remains an industry leader, but its 25 percent annual growth rates, which it enjoyed throughout the 1990s, have slipped to between 10 percent and 15 percent. Despite its continued financial strength, this slip has prompted shareholders to revolt over issues such as CEO compensation, corporate governance, and poison pill antitakeover measures.

■ Other leaders, including General Electric, AIG, and ExxonMobil, have struggled through individual ups and downs but have managed to hold onto their industry leadership positions.

The message is that nothing is guaranteed. Even companies that once seemed impervious to cracks are susceptible to failure. The real growth challenge is not just to build a growth engine that keeps a company on high ground for a few years, but rather to create a sustainable, finely tuned growth machine that lasts for decades.

POSITIVE ASPECTS OF GROWTH

Growth creates many rewards, and a lack of it will eventually—and inevitably—be costly: It's a straightforward equation. But the nature of growth in today's business environment is not as simple. Without understanding the characteristics of growth, achieving it becomes that much more difficult.

Growth Is Always Possible

Successful, profitable, Value-Building Growth is always possible—in any phase of the business cycle, in every industry, and in any geographic region. There are no excuses for not being able to grow. More than once, we've listened to clients describe their astonishment in watching their peers and competitors grow beyond expectations. They ask us how Southwest Airlines grows when the rest of the industry teeters on bankruptcy. They ask us where Nucor came from to overtake the long-standing leaders of the steel industry. And they ask us how Progressive Insurance transformed the automotive insurance market so profoundly.

In mature industries, the expectation is that most companies perform within 4 percent, above or below, the industry average. The reality, however, is that double-digit growth differences can be the rule, not the exception. Consider the airline industry: Is it true that the industry is growing at an average of only about 3 percent per year? Yes, it is. Does it mean that all players must accept this and not try to break out of a 4 percent range? No! *Range breakers,* including Southwest, Ryanair, and SkyWest, redefined the limits of their industry and managed to grow faster than the average. Such players are so aggressive that they force the competition into a steep downturn, if not directly into bankruptcy, which in turn forces the industry growth rate down.

True, the airline industry is known for its breakout companies, but in many other industries, identifying growth stars is not as easy. With our database, however, we found growth examples in every industry—and even managed to surprise some long-time CEOs of blue chip companies with our findings. Many of these companies, after all, have not made it onto the covers of major business publications. But they do exist, they are growing, and they offer valuable growth lessons.

We can see the paradox of growth mind-sets whenever there is a downturn in the automotive industry. Growth-oriented companies such as Toyota, Honda, and BMW continue to invest for the future. They expand into new growth markets, or they change their product mix to appeal to higher growing segments. Despite the short-term challenges, they relentlessly focus on growth. On the other hand, many of their competitors turn their backs on growth. They try to ride out the downturn through layoffs, plant closures, restructuring, and pruning back product lines. When demand finally picks up again, their troops are battle-weary and unable to rekindle the growth spirit.

Finally, as we discussed in Chapter 3, different regions and countries influence corporate performance through various regulatory environments, taxes, competitive laws, and levels of deregulation, but nowhere have we found an environment adverse enough to hamper significant Value-Building Growth.

Growth Has a Positive Effect on Morale and Culture

Beyond the strong correlation between growth and higher share prices, growth is also a means of fostering a winning corporate culture. Growth creates new jobs and new opportunities for employees. A growing company becomes more attractive to new or prospective employees as well as to possible alliance partners. A growing company also has an easier time of building brand equity than its competitors.

Think about how much fun it must be to work at a fast-growing, energetic company such as eBay. Or a proven industry leader like General Electric. Employees of growth companies have a spring in their step, they aren't daunted by the odd setback, and they look forward to the exciting prospects of the future.

There Is No One-Size-Fits-All Growth

Every company has its optimal growth rate that is influenced by its ability to generate cash and profits, attract new employees and leaders, expand current business without overstretching the company, and maintain a flexible organizational structure. But this rate is not fixed and, over time, companies can learn to raise it to new levels.

Microsoft, for example, currently achieves annual growth rates of around 15 percent to 20 percent, driven primarily by product upgrades and peripheral products and services to its core offerings. The company continues to be the industry leader, but this growth rate is considerably lower than when it was an innovation leader, penetrating new markets.

Sometimes, however, companies surpass their optimal growth rates and burn out. This phenomenon was rampant a few years ago during the Internet boom, but faded considerably during the recession. Remember how fast companies such as Ariba and i2 staffed up to meet the overwhelming demand they anticipated in the late 1990s? When it didn't materialize, they had to radically restructure. Today, the companies that managed to survive are a small fraction of their former size.

Growth Is Dynamic

Growth—for all companies—is dynamic over time. In other words, no company can stay on top forever. Although a stable position in the value-grower quadrant is ideal, no company in our research has been able to achieve this consistently over time. There are natural ebbs and flows, even where growth is concerned. Reasons for a slide include everything from a big merger to a market decline, but it may also be caused by suboptimal growth management. The trick is knowing how to ride out the downturns and take advantage of the upswings.

Mattel, the market share leader in the toy industry, has many ups and downs, primarily because of the fickle nature of its customers. But if one product launch is not successful, it simply moves forward with the next one. It continuously focuses on innovation and growth, recognizing that its growth rate from one year to the next may rise and fall.

Still, short of being able to stay in the value-growing quadrant, there is a next-best pattern that companies should try to emulate. This pattern takes the shape of a spiral, as the company moves from the value-growing quadrant to the simple-grower quadrant that focuses on revenue growth. In terms of management strategies, it is best to pursue revenue growth even when the market fails to see the immediate value.

Internal and External Growth Are Equally Important

The debate over internal growth versus external growth has raged in boardrooms for years. But strong proponents for either side will never be able to claim victory because sustained, superior growth relies on a mix of both.

Most value growers use both external and internal strategies to succeed. In fact, our research suggests that the most successful growth companies achieve about 60 percent of their growth through internal initiatives and 40 percent through external ones. These leading growth companies tend to avoid large, troublesome *merger of equal* acquisitions, preferring to acquire smaller companies that can easily be integrated into their core businesses. In subsequent chapters of this book, we look at how companies such as Johnson & Johnson and Nestlé balance their growth between external and internal growth initiatives.

True, there are also rare examples of successful companies that continue to focus on one strategy or the other, but this number is constantly in decline. When we looked at the combination of internal and external growth, we discovered that the necessity for external growth has increased dramatically over the past decade. The increased competitiveness of the global marketplace continues to pressure companies to grow quickly, forcing them to look beyond internal strategies that yield slower returns. External growth, primarily through acquisitions, enables companies to accelerate their growth, even though the integration benefits are not always as easy to attain as companies think.

THE IMPACT OF INDUSTRY CONSOLIDATION

Against the backdrop of a company's desire and strategies to grow lies an unstoppable business force: industry consolidation. It is imperative that a company's growth plans account for, and anticipate, this phenomenon.

In the introduction to this book, we summarized our Endgames Curve, the four stages of industry consolidation. If a company is in one of the first two stages (opening and scale), it must position itself for the inevitable consolidation wave. A strong organic growth engine is particularly important so the company can continue to gain market share at the expense of competitors, without having to make acquisitions if the timing is not right. In the third stage (focus) and fourth stage (balance and alliance) of consolidation, the competitive landscape is already crowded. Here, companies are more likely to include a well-chosen megamerger as an integral part of their growth plans.

To illustrate how industry consolidation shapes the growth strategies of companies in the various stages of industry consolidation, consider the contrast between the banking and tobacco industries. The global banking industry is the least consolidated industry in the world. Although there seems to be a new merger announcement every day, the vast majority of industry consolidation has occurred in individual countries, not internationally.

However, the future landscape for the industry suggests a 5- to 10-year period of rapid cross-border consolidation. We predict that the top three global competitors will increase their combined total market share from 10 percent today to roughly 45 percent 10 years from now. Although it is difficult to say exactly when this consolidation wave will commence or what will trigger it, when leading banks embark on international growth strategies, their competitors will not be able to stand idle. It is imperative for any bank to have a solid internal growth engine and globally competitive cost position, but it is equally imperative for banks to draw up a wish list of acquisition targets to be able to leapfrog ahead on the consolidation landscape. Also, scenario planning and war-gaming sessions are helpful techniques to plan a competitive response to potential mergers among industry rivals. The bottom line for banks is that a period of rapid consolidation is approaching and must be factored into growth strategies going forward.

The global tobacco industry, on the other hand, is one of the most concentrated and consolidated industries in the world. Aside from the controversy surrounding smoking, the industry provides a fascinating study in growth. There are essentially four significant global competitors: Altria (formerly Philip Morris), R.J. Reynolds, BAT, and Japan Tobacco. Consolidation has already occurred, and growth options are extremely limited because of the fallout on several fronts: health-related bans on advertising and promotion, steep payments to federal and state governments to pay for health problems in the United States, high taxes, and class-action and individual lawsuits brought by smokers. Beyond these problems, tobacco companies that have opted for diversification into other industries are also fumbling because any related companies or businesses are also subject to claims from lawsuits.

These constraints limit the tobacco industry's growth levers. The industry has tried to develop healthier smoking products, but even these efforts have been stymied. Case in point: the recent litigation over "light" cigarettes. The only success here would be a smoke-free cigarette that did not affect a smoker's health in any way—an unlikely prospect. Beyond this, the industry's only growth option appears to be to expand geographically, primarily into China and India, which are the two most populated and underpenetrated countries in the world. The remainder of the industry's business focus is directed toward maximizing cash to pay out the proceeds to shareholders (in the form of higher than average dividends), governments (in the form of fines and taxes), and employees (wages in the tobacco industry are always above average).

WATCHING FOR THE PITFALLS OF GROWTH

Identifying a company's strengths tends to be the easy part in preparing for growth because they are the company's core capabilities. The trick is to determine which challenges and red flags will require management attention. In any discussion about growth, there are always skeptics and naysayers who question the assumptions and logic of a growth strategy. Their comments and criticisms usually begin with the phrase, "Yes, but . . ."

Although the list of potential problem areas is long, a select few rise to the forefront time and time again. We list them here so you can use them to screen your growth plans for obvious holes and deficiencies:

- *Geographic barriers:* The decision to expand operations geographically can be a make-or-break decision, particularly for small and medium-size companies. Expansion can soak up cash and management attention, and the risks may be significant. It requires experienced internal leadership, which may or may not be available, and obtaining new and trustworthy external partners, who can often be difficult to find. And it requires meticulous planning and implementation. The question is: Is your company good at these things and prepared to accept these heightened risks?

- *Growth culture:* Culture and the attitude of the senior management team toward growth can also be a barrier. Are there in-fighting or power struggles among the senior leaders? What happens to leaders who attempt growth and fail? Who gets credit when growth is achieved? Is it one individual or an entire team? Do people think of finite growth opportunities and product or service extensions as the answer to growth, or are they encouraged to think out of the box? The answers to these questions can help determine whether your company's culture promotes or impedes growth.

- *The hockey stick business plan:* Hockey sticks often appear more frequently in business strategies than on skating rinks.

(continued)

This expression for an overly optimistic growth projection on a line chart is rooted in the belief that business conditions will be better tomorrow than they are today. When analyzing a potential growth problem or idea, a new concept might appear to be the panacea that promises to solve everything. Management teams that endorse a hockey stick projection have often failed to challenge the assumptions in its plan or failed to accurately assess its implementation capabilities. Instead, resources are often allocated to incorrect, or at least suboptimal, channels. Tough decisions must be made, and a plan for implementing these decisions is critical.

- *The forecasting dilemma:* Planning, sourcing, production, back-office operations, and sales all depend on realistic growth forecasts. But companies often experience problems because of unrealistic or misaligned forecasting processes. Companies need to invest in their forecasting systems, stress-test them, and conduct sensitivity analyses. They need to corroborate sales-driven, market-facing forecasts against supply-driven production forecasts. Otherwise, forecasts run the risk of being overly optimistic (remember the hockey stick warning), resulting in an overproduction that may have to be flooded into the market at discount prices. Conversely, if growth is not a priority and the salesforce is the only driver of the forecast, sales projections may grow only moderately, with salespeople achieving their targets and reaping their bonuses without real growth.

- *The IT barrier:* We don't have enough IT horsepower. We have the wrong IT capabilities. We have new IT that nobody understands. Do any of these complaints sound familiar? It's not too surprising that the IT infrastructure might be a growth barrier. IT is always fraught with problems and can often be used as an excuse for not being able to grow. Never-ending IT implementations and rigid process models force the business into an IT-process chokehold that strangles growth. On the other hand, as we discuss later in the book, technology has the power to open up breakthrough growth opportunities.

■ *Growth catalysts and leadership:* Companies stuck in a rut of slow or no growth may have forgotten how good growth makes employees feel. Which of your employees and leaders can rally a team around a growth initiative? Who has optimism and a can-do attitude? These individuals may be the ones to lead your next growth projects.

■ *Mergers and acquisitions:* The M&A question is one "Yes, but . . ." that may not have been raised enough in recent years. Yet M&As can be a difficult and highly political decision to make. Remember how much controversy and in-fighting the Hewlett-Packard takeover of Compaq produced? Opponents generally exaggerate the expense and integration challenges, whereas proponents tend to overestimate the strategic benefits and synergies. The trick is to maintain an even keel throughout the process, making the best decision on the known facts.

THE GROWTH DIAGNOSTIC

We have already examined how to assess your company's starting point on the road to Value-Building Growth. In the next part of the book, we explore in detail how to build a growth engine. Before we begin that leg of the growth journey, however, we run through a brief diagnostic exercise that can help you take stock of where you are in your growth strategy today. This three-step exercise is useful because you can refer to it throughout the remainder of the book, see where to improve, and identify opportunities to replicate the success of the best-practice companies outlined in our examples.

1. Determine the Minimum Required Growth Rate

Finding the minimum growth rate for your company depends on four elements: the industry's organic growth rate, factors related to industry consolidation (where the industry lies on the Endgames

Curve), the company's competitive position, and shareholder expectations.

For example, the automotive parts supplier industry has a natural growth rate of about 2 percent. However, the top three industry leaders hold a combined market share of 25 percent, and following the logic of the Endgames Curve, this should rise to roughly 40 percent over the decade. This means that if a middle-tier competitor does not want to lose relative market share against the top players, it must grow well above the industry's 2 percent natural growth rate to maintain parity with industry leaders as consolidation continues.

Another outcome of this minimum growth rate analysis may be that the company does not have a realistic chance to survive independently in the long term. If the starting position is too weak, if shareholder expectations are too optimistic, or if the minimum growth rate is too high, the company is either likely to be acquired or to experience lower than expected financial performance. In any case, this analysis is a helpful starting point for setting your company's growth targets.

2. Assess Current Growth Initiatives

Is your company well positioned for growth, or is it in immediate danger? The answer to this question, in part, will determine how well your current growth initiatives are working. Before embarking on a new series of growth strategies, companies should take stock of existing strategies. Ideally, these programs are well documented and include details about the tactical and strategic objectives, managing staff, resource allocation, current status, historical track record of similar growth initiatives, risk assessment, and an implementation time frame. This last element may be the most important. It is necessary to have a solid understanding of the time requirements of all ongoing growth initiatives; for example, which initiatives will yield results this year, which come into fruition next year, how many are long-term initiatives, and what your acquisition targets are. You must also be able to predict how industry consolidation may play out and determine what op-portunities (or threats) may result.

This overview should give you a better sense of the state of growth in your company as well as the prospects for future growth. Is the company being aggressive enough? Does growth seem to be a priority? Are top people driving key growth initiatives?

3. Identify the Growth Gap

Calculating the difference between the results from Step 1 and Step 2 will yield your company's growth gap. The size of the gaps for each of the different business units will indicate the level of strategic change that may be necessary. An example of how you might map this out is illustrated in Figure 5.1. There will be gaps

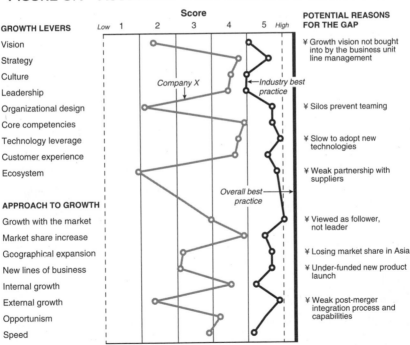

FIGURE 5.1   ASSESSING YOUR COMPANY'S GROWTH GAP

Source: A.T. Kearney.

that can realistically be closed and those that cannot. For example, in some cases it is better to divest a business and use the proceeds to increase growth in the remaining business units.

For businesses that warrant saving and can be made successful through increased growth, closing the growth gap will be a challenge. It may require difficult or unpleasant moves, raising capital, or changing long-standing company practices. Many companies have short-term growth potential that can be activated simply by removing a few operational barriers. These barriers are often well known among many employees and are, therefore, easy to find. Using a customized internal questionnaire to identify such obstacles is often a great way to spark growth.

For mid-term growth potential, it is important to derive the growth necessities coming from the market. This can be accomplished by benchmarking products and competitors, with an eye toward understanding your current growth program and how well it fulfills the market's growth necessities.

Finding a successful long-term strategy is the silver bullet for future performance. Conventional methods and standard analyses are not enough. The answer lies in the pages ahead. As you read through the rest of this book, try to gauge the magnitude of change required in your company against the case studies of companies with similar growth gaps.

In this part, we have demonstrated the important benefits that can be derived from growth and offered assessment tools for a first-cut analysis to assess your internal *state of growth* and your company's position in its industry. The next part of this book is the heart of solving the growth challenge. We present four key steps to building your company's growth engine, using several case studies to illustrate these steps. Some of the cases are of well-known companies, which you will recognize immediately, while others are fairly new. Regardless of where your company is today, the next part should give you plenty of ideas and inspiration to accelerate your growth.

PART III

THE STRETCH GROWTH MODEL

CHAPTER 6

Introduction to the Stretch Growth Model

During the Enlightenment, French philosopher the Marquis de Condorcet embraced the idea that humankind is infinitely perfectible. In his book, *The Future Progress of the Human Mind,* he wrote, "The progress of [humankind's] perfectibility . . . has no other limit than the duration of the globe upon which nature has placed us." The same holds true for today's corporations: The possibility to perfect growth is limitless.

As we've said, most CEOs recognize that their companies are not achieving their full growth potential. But many are unsure how—and where—to tap into it. The fact is, growth opportunities are everywhere—in every office, department, function, and business unit of every company and across all links of the value chain. At its best, a company can be viewed as a growth machine: All functions, all categories produce growth in one way or another.

How does this happen? Our research and experience show that most companies begin to grow primarily by removing operational and structural barriers, and then by stretching one or more of their core strengths. Companies that achieve superior results are able to reach new heights in all aspects of their business— satisfying customers, delivering a high-quality product or service, achieving a low-cost position, building a team of motivated top-performing employees, and—most importantly—making money.

When we looked more closely at the thousands of companies in our database, we began to notice some specific patterns. We were able to discern hierarchies of growth initiatives; some growth strategies achieved benefits more easily than others. The result of this observation is a comprehensive model that helps companies stretch every aspect of their growth potential (see Figure 6.1). The four stages are:

1. Operations.
2. Organization.
3. Strategy.
4. Stretch.

Most companies excel at one, or even several, growth drivers in each stage, but to be truly successful, companies must master all of them. Only then will they begin to see a quantum increase in business performance.

Moving through the four stages of the stretch growth model leads companies to new heights of business performance. Companies that progress through the stages logically will achieve maximum business impact as quickly and easily as possible, while at the same time limiting exposure to risk. In line with this, the strategies across the four stages begin with the basics and become increasingly sophisticated. To illustrate the many sides of the stretch model, consider the different approaches of two of Canada's most successful food retailers, Metro (formerly Metro-Richelieu) and Loblaw's.

A TALE OF TWO STRATEGIES

Metro, Canada's third-largest food retailer, is an excellent example of the operations aspect of the stretch model. With a company

FIGURE 6.1 THE STRETCH GROWTH MODEL

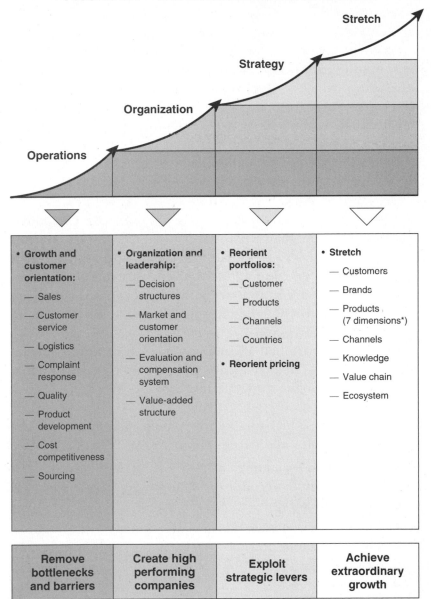

Encompasses: solutions, service, speed, convenience, microsegmentation, results orientation, and risk sharing.
Source: A.T. Kearney.

motto of "Retail is detail," Metro's emphasis on operations excellence is the core of its success.

Metro is a regional food retailer that has built its reputation on excellent operations, low prices, high quality, and a satisfying shopping experience. Metro's business is primarily in the Canadian province of Quebec, and for the past six years, it has been under siege from all sides. Wal-Mart, Costco, and other American superstores have invaded from the south; Loblaw's, Canada's largest food retailer, has attacked from the west; and Sobey's, another large Canadian food retailer, has entered the Quebec market from the east.

Despite this onslaught, Metro has achieved fantastic results. Revenues have increased over the past six years at a compound annual rate of more than 5 percent. This stands in stark contrast to a 2 percent industry average in the region and is higher than any other established competitor. Metro's profit margins have averaged almost 2 percent, 60 basis points higher than the industry average, and Metro's ROE has averaged 25 percent, versus an industry average of 15 percent.

How has Metro pulled off such numbers in the face of brutal competition? It has adopted an obsessive approach to operational excellence. Some of its strategies include:

- Emphasizing high-quality fresh foods, deli selections, and prepared meals—all in areas where Wal-Mart can't compete.

- Continually evaluating and readjusting store locations and retail footprint to account for changing demographics and consumer behavior.

- Turning its wholesale business with independent retailers, hotels, restaurants, hospitals, and schools into a powerhouse so it can reduce distribution costs to the bone and stay on top of consumer trends.

- Making senior executives *live* the business. As one colleague of Metro CEO, Pierre Lessard, explains, "On a rainy weekend, [Pierre] will take me to [rural Quebec] to check out the price of green peas at our competitors' stores."

On the other end of the stretch growth model is Loblaw's. As Canada's largest food retailer, Loblaw's expanded on its operational excellence by using a combination of innovation and acquisitions, and in doing so, it has become a stellar example of a stretch company.

Since its doors first opened in 1919, Loblaw's has evolved into a retailing powerhouse, with annual revenues of more than US$13 billion. Loblaw's operates more than 2,000 company-owned and franchised stores. Revenues have grown more than 15 percent compounded annually over the past five years, with profits growing more than 18 percent annually.

The senior management team of Loblaw's has taken the company from its roots as a food retailer and stretched its concept and mandate in every conceivable direction:

- *Geographic expansion:* Loblaw's has expanded geographically both organically and through acquisitions. Originally an Ontario-based food retailer, Loblaw's has expanded across Canada to become the leading national retailer.

- *Brand expansion:* Loblaw's was a global pioneer in using its strength in food retailing to build a consumer products franchise. In the late 1980s and early 1990s, Loblaw's branded and marketed its own private-label products under the banners "PC" and "President's Choice." President's Choice became synonymous with high-quality, reasonably priced products— and turned into a staple brand of Canadian households. For Loblaw's, this translates into the fact that 29 percent of its sales come from its private-label goods; for U.S. food retailers, the average stands at just 13 percent. This favorable sales mix results in bigger margins for Loblaw's. In fact, the President's Choice brand has proven so successful that Loblaw's has licensed it to other retailers around the world.

- *Store format expansion:* As Canada's largest food retailer, Loblaw's found itself under competitive pressure from players such as Wal-Mart, various regional Canadian grocers, pharmacies, and even gasoline retailers. To maintain its dominance and repel competition, Loblaw's became proficient at competing in any type of retail format. It opened no-frills stores to compete against rock-bottom-priced competitors. It also transformed many of its stores to position them as one-stop shopping destinations, offering dry-cleaning services, wine and beer sales, a full range of pharmacy products, and photo processing.

■ *Stretching brand expansion:* In keeping with its one-stop shopping concept, Loblaw's entered into a partnership with Amicus, a subsidiary of the Canadian Imperial Bank of Commerce, in 1998 to provide basic financial services to Loblaw's customers right at the store. The idea took off, and the partnership has since launched President's Choice-branded credit cards, savings accounts, a loyalty points program, mortgages, and, most recently, a new line of index mutual funds.

■ *Stretching store format expansion:* Loblaw's recently announced that it plans to storm into yet another area by operating gasoline stations. At a shareholders' meeting, Loblaw's president, John Lederer, observed that because so many of Loblaw's customers come to their stores in cars, providing gas "seemed a natural format extension."

At every step along the way, Loblaw's has taken risks and used innovative ideas to reach beyond traditional boundaries. Never afraid to try something new and rarely unsuccessful with new products and services, Loblaw's exemplifies what it means to be an industry leader—and a stretch company.

As the comparison between Metro and Loblaw's illustrates, there are many different angles and approaches for creating growth in your company. We go deeper into these by previewing the key aspects of each stage of the stretch growth model.

1. Operations: Cleaning House

The first step on the growth journey is to do some operational housecleaning. As with regular housecleaning, it's never fully done. In fact, we have yet to encounter a company that has achieved full, 100 percent operational efficiency. The downside is that the constant struggle can resemble a Sisyphean struggle. The upside is that there's always room for improvement, even if such opportunities are generally found in seemingly mundane areas. Companies that overlook the growth potential in operations do so at their own expense. In fact, A.T. Kearney's research indicates that the operations improvements we discuss here can account for 60 percent or more of a company's future growth potential, and, of the four growth steps, the operations step is the easiest to implement.

The key areas we focus on include:

- *Sourcing and vendor management:* The decisions surrounding purchasing goods and services account for 20 percent to 60 percent of the cost structure of industrial companies and as much as 80 percent to 90 percent for retailers and wholesalers. And when a company optimizes its sourcing process, it can reduce a company's total costs anywhere from 6 percent to 13 percent. It may not sound sexy, but it is profitable.

- *Product and service quality:* During his tenure at General Electric, Jack Welch brought Six Sigma and total quality management to the business world, but companies continue to struggle with achieving consistently superior product and service quality. Drawing on examples from the global travel industry, we underscore the significant impact that improving quality can have on a company.

- *New product development:* A robust innovation pipeline holds the key to a company's future. After all, what sells well today may be obsolete tomorrow. Think of Polaroid. Once a leading company in the photography industry, it was unable to keep up with changing technology and customer demands and fell into bankruptcy in 2001. On the flip side, companies that place a premium on innovation—from 3M to Mercedes-Benz—know that a steady focus on creating tomorrow's products and services is a cornerstone for growth.

■ *On-time delivery:* Everyone knows time is money, yet more than one-third of the companies we researched experienced issues with punctuality. Shoring up the delivery process not only prevents unnecessary losses, but is a relatively easy and low-risk area to achieve measurable improvement. And in some industries, there is a considerable gap between industry leaders and laggards.

Consider the mortgage industry, for example. In the United States, interest rates are at an all-time low. But even for people with good credit, who pose little risk, it still takes a month or more to seal the deal. The same is true in Germany. The time between filling out the paperwork and getting your euros can take up to four weeks on average. But go next door to Belgium for a loan, and you will have it in a week or less. What do the Belgians have that the Americans and Germans do not? Less bureaucracy. The Belgians have the mortgage loan process down to a science. Less paper, less process, and fewer people all add up to faster delivery.

■ *Superior customer service:* Attracting and then retaining customers is another cornerstone of growth—and an area where improved attention to detail can reap hefty rewards. One-third of the European companies we researched revealed gaps in service performance. With customer loyalty at a premium, we take a close look at some lessons offered by leading companies in the railway and hotel industry.

■ *Sales effectiveness:* The sales team is the main link between products and customers, and having the people and the processes needed to consistently clinch the good deals is critical. However, identifying potential lapses in this area is often as difficult as correcting them. Many companies can boost their bottom lines by revisiting and updating some of their key sales strategies, such as altering their compensation structures for sales teams to targeting new customer groups.

■ *Pricing strategy and execution:* Gone are the days when the market determined prices. A simple example to illustrate the point is Gillette, the world's leading maker of razors and razor blades. It brought many customers on board by subsidizing the price of razors with superior technology—and compensated with higher prices and margins on its razor blades. Companies are finding that they have considerable power and flexibility in setting new price structures—and are seeing their profits rise as a result. Importantly, companies are using new pricing models as an alternative to traditional cost-cutting strategies.

2. Organization: Structuring for Success

With the operational foundation set, the next step in our growth model is to create a solid, high-performing organizational structure. Organization-oriented growth improvements can account for another 25 percent of your company's future growth potential, but they are more difficult to implement. And, if you make a real breakthrough, like some of the companies we profile, you can hit a home run in growth just by breaking through your organization's bottlenecks. How is it that some companies are able to build organization structures that support good business decisions all the time? How do some companies make solid, well-informed decisions in a few hours, when others take days or weeks? Why is it that some companies' organizations are flexible and results-focused, while other companies continually tinker with rigid, formal organization structures and, in the process, stifle growth and creativity?

With thousands of different working parts, today's corporations are complex entities, and their inner machinations—how these various parts function together—significantly influence the company's overall success. How many companies have compensation and reward systems that do not align with market and client success? How many banks have officers dedicated to being the single point of contact for customers, assisting them with all of their needs? All too often, customers in banking—and virtually every other industry—are shuffled among various departments and employees and are easily lost in the confusion.

We anchor our discussion on this step, as we do the chapters, with case studies of companies that offer compelling lessons on how—and how not—to approach organizational strategies. Goldman Sachs, Sara Lee, and HSBC each chose different roads and met with varying degrees of success. But in many areas, they established new levels of excellence. Following even the best standard-bearers step by step will not take you to the same place. Each organization should be viewed as distinct and unique as a fingerprint: No two are exactly alike.

Still, many similarities exist, and we've identified a series of best practices that companies may use to model—and then tailor— their individual strategies:

▪ *Eliminate friction:* Friction between two departments, or even two leaders, can effectively stall growth if the problem is not quickly recognized and addressed. However, in creating the best organizational structure for their company, executives must not only find and eliminate existing points of friction or bottlenecks, but also create a structure that encourages potential and fosters success. In other words, it's not just about fixing parts that are broken or smoothing out wrinkles; it's about forging a platform for growth.

Many clashes within companies are as much a result of the organizational structure as differing ideas or personalities. When two departments are functionally separate, the different incentives or goals may inadvertently pit them against each other. Or an organization may suffer from the too-many-cooks syndrome, as did one of our clients. Under the company's matrix structure, the sales, product development, and manufacturing departments were jointly responsible for the product division. But there was a high price attached to this committee-style approach: In the end, no single person had a clear line of responsibility for the product. Thus, no one was compelled to respond to changing market conditions, internal constraints, or customer complaints. Only after implementing a team-based approach, which included shifting responsibilities and attaching clear lines to individuals and groups, was the company able to solve the problem.

■ *Break down growth barriers:* Matrix organizations, functional silos, and global business units are all organizational concepts that were popular throughout recent decades. Each of these theories has strengths—but it is important for senior management teams to be aware that they can affect growth in unexpected ways. Ask any company that's dealt with organizational silos, and they'll tell you they aren't the ideal way to grow. It is critical to remember that the key to growth is to develop supplemental or tangential processes that cut through or across rigid organization structures to unleash the power of a company's most talented people. At General Electric, Jack Welch was famous for his *workout* process and his business review meetings. Each of these concepts helped eliminate organizational inertia and kept the focus on the business issue at hand.

Improving the value chain has also become popular as a means to focus a company on its core tasks and mission. Outsourcing IT and business processes, for example, is at an all-time high in the United States and Europe. Reconfiguring the value chain, although a major initiative, can help companies reduce their overall costs, increase their flexibility, and improve their innovation rate, thus giving them a new strategic position with a better and stronger chance to grow.

■ *Improve decision-making processes:* More than once, U.S. President Harry Truman pointed to the sign on his desk that read, "The buck stops here." In today's companies, however, it's not always clear where the buck stops or how many hands it must pass through to get there. Clear and efficient decision-making processes, particularly in volatile situations, can mean the difference between profit and loss, chaos and order.

In a business environment where the potential risks and liabilities are increasing, the natural inclination for senior leaders is to rein in decision-making processes. But companies such as HSBC and Goldman Sachs prove this notion wrong.

They have found ways to keep employees empowered, and they are able to make important decisions painlessly and fast.

■ *Align compensation and growth:* In recent years, many companies have transformed their compensation systems and tied them to measures such as economic value added (EVA) and return on equity (ROE). These efforts represented attempts to motivate CEOs and senior managers to tie their compensation to increases in their company's share price. Generally, these new compensation formulas were implemented hand-in-hand with stock option grants. In hindsight, however, these schemes worked only in the short to medium term. In their wake, the relentless focus on profits and cost-cutting has left many companies with a paucity of growth prospects.

The lesson learned is that it is important to emphasize balance in a compensation system. By brainstorming the various possible outcomes or scenarios of revisions in compensation systems, companies can often foresee the unintended consequences of what had seemed like the right move. They can ensure that growth remains a top priority and that their employees are rewarded for achieving it.

3. Strategy: Pulling the Growth Levers

When executives think about the role of strategy in growth, they often think of a big strategic breakthrough that will transform their industry and result in a sales jump of tens of percentage points. But our research suggests a different course of action. Most companies, we believe, are already on the right overall strategic track. And rather than look for a miracle breakthrough, they should take a holistic view of their strategy and find specific growth opportunities within it. We call this tactic "exploiting the strategic status quo."

For some companies, exploiting the strategic status quo may lead to breakthrough results, but for most, it means redoubling their efforts on what made them strong in the first place. Consider Toyota, the leading automotive manufacturer in terms of market capitalization. Toyota's strategy is not flashy. It has achieved its top position not by a massive acquisition or a radical diversification program, but by slow and steady geographic expansion and by making low-cost, high-quality cars that people like to drive.

In our chapter on strategy (Chapter 9), we look at six strategic growth levers and discuss ways to leverage them to enhance your company's growth prospects. The best answers, however, always begin with the best questions:

- *What industry are you really in?* Most companies approach their business by looking at which companies they directly compete against but often overlook more fundamental industry dynamics. In the automotive industry, for example, would you rather be a manufacturer, stuck in a cyclical, capital-intensive, low-margin business, or in auto insurance, where companies with the best customers enjoy a high-margin business with steady profits? Looking across the entire value chain of the industry will help clarify where growth opportunities may arise and how to capitalize on them.

- *What is your customer growth strategy?* Spending time with customers and learning more about what they need and how they use various products or services can yield a goldmine of information about good opportunities for growth. Customers should be at the center of your growth strategy; their wants and needs should determine product and service offerings, how your company manages your customers' life cycle, how you serve different customer or market segments, and so on.

- *Which distribution channels fuel the best growth?* Companies often have more distribution options than they realize. In fact, there are always new ways to work better with distribution partners. In this section, we look at how to decide which distribution strategy will maximize your growth options.

- *Which countries should you compete in?* Selecting the right portfolio of countries to compete in is an important strategic decision. Critical factors include how much capital your company has available for expansion, your time frame for results, and your experience and track record in achieving growth in international markets. This section will help you to make these growth trade-offs more effectively.

■ *What is the best product portfolio?* Reshaping your product or service portfolio may sound like a tactical improvement, not a strategic one. But in our experience, companies need to work from a more strategic vantage point when deciding what products and services to offer and promote. How might your product portfolio be tailored to better meet customer needs? Do your products cannibalize one another? How well do you develop and launch new products? These are some of the strategic product portfolio questions that can lead to growth.

■ *Where do mergers and acquisitions fit in?* We save what is perhaps the most important strategic growth question—the role of mergers and acquisitions—for last. So much has been written about how mergers fail to create shareholder value and how so many companies rely too heavily on mergers to achieve growth. Despite the bad press, M&As have an important role in achieving growth, particularly for companies in industries that are rapidly consolidating.

4. Stretch: Searching for Breakthroughs

The first three stages of the stretch growth model are fairly discrete and easy to visualize, if not to implement. The fourth step, the stretch growth stage, is more creative. Stretch opportunities have the potential to create breakthrough growth and transform your business. But they aren't a sure-fire ticket to success, and your company must be prepared to fail.

Only a few companies in the world are able to stretch their businesses and capabilities along several dimensions simultaneously to achieve growth from a plethora of sources. These companies, such as Nestlé and Johnson & Johnson, have set the standard. But in the meantime, while you build a growth strategy based on solid oper-ations, organization, and strategic growth initiatives, there are many places in your company where a stretch growth idea might take root.

You might look at your product or service offerings to see if you have opportunities to stretch your customer base, your cus-tomer service levels, or the level of convenience and customiza-tion you provide. You might stretch your value chain or business model, your geographic reach, or your partnership and risk-sharing approach to improve growth. You might stretch the way you go to market through your distribution channel strategy or your branding. You might look to new technologies to stretch your entire company. Or, you might try to stretch in several directions at once and find the ideal combination of growth ideas that will boost your company to the next level of performance.

Even if your company is the leader in its industry, we believe you can learn from the masters of other types of businesses. For this reason, we have included more than 20 stretch growth case studies in Chapter 10.

DECENTRALIZED AND UNIFIED

To summarize the four growth stages and to illustrate some of the growth concepts we have discussed, we consider the case of a lead-ing global supplier of automotive components, Illinois Tool Works (ITW). Formed in 1912 to design and sell metal cutting tools, ITW has evolved into a global manufacturer of highly engineered products and specialty systems; it supplies the construction, food retail and service, automotive, and general industrial markets. The company's product expertise lies primarily in the areas of plastic and metal fasteners, adhesives, labeling, plastics, and electrostatic painting technology.

ITW lives by many of the principles embedded in the four growth stages. From an organizational standpoint, ITW empha-sizes a strong, experienced management team that has grown up in ITW. Despite owning a portfolio of more than 600 separate companies, ITW operates in a decentralized manner, focusing on the specific competitive dynamics and growth opportunities in each individual business unit. But it unifies its many diverse businesses through an operating principle it calls *80/20*. ITW describes this operating philosophy as follows:

> The concept underlying 80/20 is simple: 80 percent of a business' sales are derived from the 20 percent of its product offering being sold to key customers. Put simply, too often companies do not spend enough time on the critical 20 percent of their key customers and products and spend too much time on the less important 80 percent. This process is really about simplifying and focusing on the key parts of your business. Simplicity focuses action, while complexity often blurs what is important. In the process of simplification, we view all aspects of the business on an 80/20 basis. This includes finding ways to simplify our product lines, customer and supply base, and business processes and systems. In the end, 80/20 improves quality, productivity, delivery, innovation, market penetration, and ultimately, customer satisfaction.[1]

From a strategy standpoint, 70 percent of ITW's 2002 revenues of US$9.5 billion were from businesses where ITW is the industry leader. The company believes that this position of strength allows it to get closer to its customers than any other competitor and, as a result, lead their industries in design, cost competitiveness, and innovation. In addition, ITW uses acquisitions aggressively to attain and reinforce industry leadership. It breaks its acquisition strategy into two types: *bottom-up* business unit-driven acquisitions, which average approximately 30 deals per year, and *top-down* corporate-driven, strategic acquisitions, which represent only four completed deals since 1986. ITW has relied on smaller, bottom-up deals because they are cheaper, almost immediately accretive to earnings, less risky, and easier to integrate.

The results of ITW's stretch growth strategy have been phenomenal. Over the past 25 years, the company has achieved a compound annual growth rate in revenue of 15 percent, growth in

FIGURE 6.2 GLOBAL CONGLOMERATE INDUSTRY

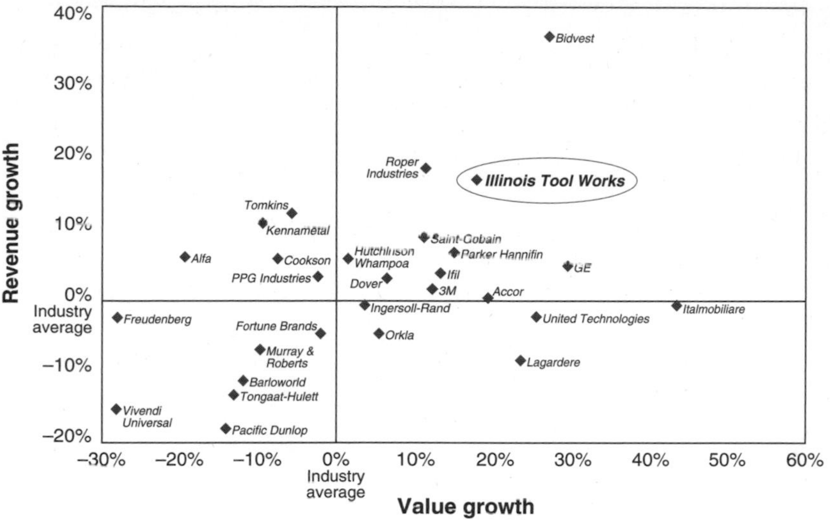

Note: Growth portfolio (CAGR 1996–2002) benchmarked against industry average.
Source: A.T. Kearney.

earnings per share of 13 percent, and growth in shareholder returns of 19 percent. And ITW has led its competitors and maintained its position in the value-growing quadrant over the past five years (see Figure 6.2).

With performances like ITW's to inspire us, let's dive into the details of the four stages of growth: operations, organization, strategy, and *stretch*.

CHAPTER 7

Operations: Removing Bottlenecks and Barriers

The first growth step may not seem like a creative or strategic move at all. If anything, it's as mundane as sweeping the floor. And in many ways, that's just what it is. But for all the overwrought metaphors of creating a solid foundation and of getting your house in order, the idea holds true: Without mastering the basics, there's little hope of excelling at more complex strategies. Our research underscores this at every turn: Companies that achieve superior growth are operational powerhouses.

Admittedly, in the beginning, this realization seems counterintuitive. More often than not, growth initiatives are deemed strategic and not operational. In fact, of the companies and industries we've examined, roughly 75 percent of all growth potential is hidden within short- and mid-term operations projects. The remaining 25 percent—still a significant portion—is uncovered in longer term strategic initiatives. Positioning a company for growth through operational improvements holds little risk and produces significant, solid benefits. Strategic breakthroughs can produce the odd home run but will most likely fail if the solid operational backbone is not in place.

And if there's any lingering desire to skip this chapter, consider how few companies can lay claim to operational excellence. In our experience, there aren't many. In almost every company we've studied and worked with, operational bottlenecks, in one form or another, either inhibit growth or prevent it altogether.

Knowing how to pinpoint—and then clear—these operational bottlenecks creates the necessary foundation for growth. To illustrate this point, we look at perhaps the world's most successful operations-focused growth company, Wal-Mart.

OPERATIONS-DRIVEN GROWTH AT WAL-MART

The success of Wal-Mart's growth model is legendary. The company has grown from a single store in a remote part of the United States to become the largest, most powerful retailer in the world. But at the core of Wal-Mart's success lies a single message: Create a simple business model that provides consumers with the products they want at rock-bottom prices.

Wal-Mart has been able to leverage and replicate its core strengths: its process for selecting new store locations, its vendor negotiation and relationship management process, and its supply chain management systems. The powerful concept behind these strengths is that as Wal-Mart grows, the strengths are reinforced. The bigger Wal-Mart becomes, the greater its purchasing power and economies of scale in its supply chain. This means it can continuously improve its cost position and offer even lower prices to consumers, which in turn allows it to increase market share and start the growth process again. Essentially, Wal-Mart's business model allows it to become even stronger as it expands its business. It is a powerful growth engine.

Wal-Mart also embraces many other traits of operationally excellent growth companies. It capitalizes on the consolidation of its supplier industries. In fact, Wal-Mart is so big that it regularly accounts for one-third, or more, of the sales revenue of consumer products giants such as Procter & Gamble and Mattel. Through high-impact training programs and by tying employee rewards to its own financial performance, Wal-Mart has developed a highly skilled and effective workforce while other companies, notably fast-food giant McDonald's, have failed.

Importantly, Wal-Mart does not use acquisitions as a crutch for growth. Rather, it acquires companies only as a tactical tool for entering new geographies more quickly than it could by pursuing internally-funded growth. Its acquisition of Asda, Britain's food and clothing superstore, is a perfect example of its strategy, having acquired 259 stores and 19 depots across the United Kingdom. Wal-Mart's supply chain operations are also world-class: It continually reengineers its supply chain to achieve maximum product availability with minimal inventory, short lead times, and low costs.

The bottom line on Wal-Mart is that it constantly—if not relentlessly—capitalizes on its operational core competencies as the basis for its growth.

We turn now to seven of the most important operational growth levers that can be used to improve your company's growth performance.

1. SOURCING AND VENDOR MANAGEMENT

The decision processes around vendor selection, payment, and working relationships may seem unrelated to the issue of growth, but it is. In fact, purchased materials are responsible for roughly 20 percent to 60 percent of the cost structure of industrial companies; the number soars to 80 percent to 90 percent for wholesalers and retailers. Original equipment manufacturers (OEMs), such as GM and General Electric, and retailers, such as Wal-Mart and Home Depot, live and die by virtue of their sourcing advantages.

In this light, best-in-class purchasing is a major cost lever and a potential survival tool for companies. In addition, it is important for ensuring high quality and using the know-how of the suppliers in the development of new products.

A.T. Kearney's client work is a consistent and profound demonstration that optimizing the sourcing process (also known as *strategic sourcing*) can reduce a company's total costs anywhere from 6 percent to 13 percent. These benefits are relatively painless—they do not involve headcount reduction programs or massive write-offs. And, more important, the benefits derived from strategic sourcing can create the financial flexibility with which to create growth:

- Companies can reinvest their cost savings into growth programs, including developing new products or services or programs to improve quality.

- Companies can take advantage of a reduced cost structure to compete more effectively against lower cost competitors.

- As unit costs are lowered, companies can increase revenues, enjoy greater pricing flexibility, and gain competitive advantage.

When Japanese automakers stormed the Western market in the mid-1980s, they trumped their competitors on all fronts: price, quality, customer service, and delivery time. In response, U.S. automakers embarked on global sourcing strategies, followed by quality and service campaigns. The cost reductions they gained through their sourcing initiatives not only helped them regain lost footing, but ultimately sparked the restructuring of the entire industry.

One of the more interesting stories that emerged from this upheaval involves the rise of GM's Blue Macaw. Blue Macaw is the unofficial name of GM's innovative modular assembly plant that opened in southern Brazil in 2000, in which 17 suppliers come together to one location to build the cars. By working with its suppliers in such a collaborative, creative way, GM has created a model that others are scrambling to replicate. Competitors have watched closely as Blue Macaw—with 90 percent automation—is able to assemble a car in two minutes. Ford, for example, has plans to open its own "supplier manufacturing campus" in 2004, which will include a broad mix of suppliers.

2. PRODUCT AND SERVICE QUALITY

In the post-TQM and Six Sigma era, it might be tempting to assume that quality is a given. But consumer research reveals that a satisfied customer will recommend a company to between two and five people, while an unhappy customer will pass on the message to 20 or more people. Making sure that your company really delivers high-quality products or services can be an important growth lever. A high-quality product can increase customer retention rates and steal market share from poorer-performing competitors. For examples of both exceptional and decidedly lackluster performance in quality, look no further than punctuality in the global travel industry.

In the airline industry, even the most patriotic Italians find fault with Alitalia because of the company's notoriously poor on-time record. At the other end, there is Singapore Airlines, which is one of the fastest growing airlines, in large part because of its exemplary punctuality record. Meanwhile, Lufthansa, even after considerable turmoil with German air traffic controllers over the past several years, still boasts incredible customer loyalty because of its solid record of on-time performance.

Germany's Deutsche Bahn has been working to improve its record for the past two years. Its goal is to reach the best-in-class standards that Japan's Shinkansen has set. For example, it is trying to improve its rail and scheduling systems and combine its cargo and passenger lines. By improving its punctuality alone, Deutsche Bahn could increase its overall revenues by 3 percent to 6 percent. So far, however, it has had mixed results.

In the automotive industry, Toyota enjoys both high revenues and strong stock price performance year after year, in large part because of its consistent top-quality ratings. Achieving similar levels of quality has become a priority for its competitors. For example, among the first measures Dieter Zetsche implemented in his restructuring campaign for Chrysler was to guarantee that Chrysler would be imbued with the famous Daimler quality. Bob Lutz boosted sales at Ford several years ago in Germany by announcing an unconditional three-year warranty for all cars—with immediate effect on the revenues. He is currently focusing on developing exciting new product lines in his current role at GM.

3. NEW PRODUCT DEVELOPMENT

New product or service development can form the cornerstone of a company's growth strategy. Consider 3M, inventors of useful—and ubiquitous—products such as tapes, adhesives, and Post-It Notes. The company's entire growth strategy is based on continuous innovation and launching new products. In fact, new products account for roughly one-third of its revenues. With a culture that fosters creativity and gives employees the freedom to take risks, 3M has churned out more than 50,000 innovative products.

In a similar example, a large American medical supply company suffered from a disconnect between its scientists and its marketing department: The scientists developed products for which there was little market demand, which left the marketers with the unhappy chore of promoting products to an apathetic marketplace. On the flip side, there are benefits when the product development process hits all the right notes and key processes are linked. Consider the great success story of the decades-old partnerships between Mercedes-Benz and Bosch. Working together, they developed a series of new braking systems. In 1978, they created the antilock braking system, which has since become standard in all Mercedes-Benz cars. More recently, they invented the Electronic Stability Program® that reduces skidding due to icy or wet road conditions. The series of products has helped make Mercedes-Benz a world-renowned leader for its comprehensive safety systems.

New products boost revenues, but they also stimulate other growth levers, such as innovation, idea sharing across business units, and cross-selling opportunities. Consider the Woolwich, a U.K. bank acquired by Barclay's in 2000. Its Open Plan offering links a customer's mortgage with other borrowing and savings products, benefiting bank and customer alike. The customer gets a lower interest rate on money borrowed and a simpler way to manage finances. At the same time, the bank has increased lifetime customer income by 65 percent, sells roughly double the national average of products per customer, and has reduced nonperforming mortgage loans.

Let's look at how some of the operational growth ideas we've covered so far are put into action in a leading pharmacy company, Walgreens.

Walgreens

Walgreens (not related to Wal-Mart), is a national retail pharmacy chain in the United States that tells a similarly compelling growth story. Founded in 1901, the company has achieved 28 consecutive years of record sales and profits. Over the past five years, it has grown revenues at an average of 16 percent per year and profits at an average of 18 percent.

In keeping with the theme of operations excellence as the foundation for strong growth, Walgreens' web site offers the following comments about its business strategy: "[Our strategy is] not particularly fancy, but it's a rock-solid approach." The cornerstones of its growth model are basic and clear:

- Invest heavily in technology and supply chain to keep service levels up and costs down. Walgreens has been a leader in using technology to build competitive advantages. In 1981, for example, it connected all of its pharmacies via satellite to better manage inventory and monitor consumer buying habits and trends. It also led the industry in point-of-sale scanning and in optimizing pharmacist workflow.

- Dominate local markets through a three-pronged strategy: "Dense up," or heavily saturate target areas with stores; relocate to continually optimize the best locations as a target neighborhood changes and evolves; and remodel stores to provide added convenience for consumers and a fresh look.

- Focus on customer convenience. As Walgreens says, "Every corner of Walgreens' strategy is focused on convenience: how fast people get into the store—or are served in the drive-thru pharmacy . . . how fast they get out . . . how easily they find what they came to buy . . . and, how well we remind them of what they are forgetting to buy."

- Avoid the distraction and financial risk of acquisitions, and instead focus on the core strengths of its business.

4. ON-TIME DELIVERY

With quality ensured, the next step is delivery. Again, delivery is often overlooked as an area for improvement, yet more than one-third of companies that we examined struggled with various delivery issues. FedEx could write the book on the importance of being on time. As the world's leading express package delivery company, FedEx handles more than 5.3 million shipments each day across more than 210 countries.

A leading European manufacturer of fashion eyewear enjoyed strong brand image, with trend-setting designs and high-quality products, but faltered when it came to delivery. In fact, it lost as much as 42 percent of potential revenue because of its disastrous performance for reliable delivery, a rate that stood at just 56 percent.

Japan's Kanban movement and principles of just-in-time delivery have dramatically improved the automotive and other capital goods industries, yet neither has filtered into all manufacturing industries. Consumer goods companies are particularly prone to delivery issues, partly because of styles that change with the seasons. As the manufacturing process becomes increasingly flexible and as more customers demand customized products, the delivery system will shift from a push to a pull model. The result will be more logistical demands, including 100 percent delivery reliability and speedier delivery times.

5. SUPERIOR CUSTOMER SERVICE

What does customer service get you? Loyalty and a captive audience when selling new products and services—both of which no company can afford to pass up.

Still, a full one-third of European companies suffer gaps in their customer service. Most improvements in this area begin with revisiting—and reassessing—a company's target customer groups and their needs. Often, a reassessment will reveal a flaw in the analysis. For example, a company that looks closely at how it is analyzing its customer groups may find that its target groups are too large. They encompass several groups at once and effectively keep the company from finding out about the true needs and desires of its primary customers, thereby preventing it from meeting their true needs. A business traveler, for example, is looking for a different travel experience than a family on vacation. What if railway companies tailor travel packages to the various subgroups—having gathered detailed information about travel patterns, booking priorities, and service preferences? If the information garnered in the customer survey is wrong, passengers end up being less than satisfied with their travel experience. Consider the possibilities. Someone in business class who loves children but expects to get a good two hours of work in on his laptop during a flight to Dallas may be disheartened to find a two-year-old in the next seat. Or, what if a bank started to "sell money" instead of receiving an application for a loan. Rather than cultivating the business relationship over the lifetime of the customer's loan, while adjusting to his or her changing requirements, the bank would do everything short of illegal activities to simply get the money back.

The power of customer service is exemplified by the Four Seasons Hotels group. In the 2003 annual survey conducted by J.D. Power and Associates, the Four Seasons received the highest service rating among luxury hotels. One of its secrets is to encourage all staff members to observe their guests and anticipate their needs, rather than waiting for a guest to ask for something. The chain also maintains profiles on frequent guests to track everything from room to dining preferences. By redefining the service standards in the five-star hotel segment, it changed its industry and has been rewarded with both strong revenue growth and stock price performance. The Four Seasons, however, is not alone in its quest to deliver superior service. The Hyatt chain is also delivering high-quality service at premium prices and winning equally high rewards for growth.

Companies that actively pursue customer service have the potential to change other industries as well, including how work is performed in areas from financial services and transportation to machinery and metal processing. To prove this point, we need look no further than the boom in the service industry sector.

6. SALES EFFECTIVENESS

Nearly one-quarter of the companies we researched had flawed sales processes. Pinpointing problem areas in sales can be difficult. Sometimes the wrong customers are being targeted; in other cases, there may be an imbalance between existing and new customers. Because sales is relationship-based, it is critical to set the right incentives for your salespeople. For example, if salespeople are not properly motivated to bring in new customers, they may be inclined to spend more time with existing, and more familiar, customers. In other words, all too often there is a discrepancy between these two areas, with the sales department being run independently.

Rather than a detached sales team, there should be a strong alignment between overall corporate goals and the goals established for the sales team. The compensation system should be crafted to create the right incentives—favoring commissions over high fixed salaries, for example.

Companies looking to improve their sales process would do well to take a few lessons from the various stages of the Endgames. What if companies in the opening stages adjust their sales process to one used by companies in the scale stages? For example, when the salesforce should be hungry, it is instead complacent, more like the salesforce in a state-run monopoly. Or in the opposite view, what if the railways took their cues from the travel agencies and the airlines? What if banks modeled their sales processes after the insurance industry, with its highly motivated salesforces? Could banks then make credit decisions in one week instead of one month? What if telecom companies designed their sales processes after mail-order houses, adopting their short response times, prompt deliveries, user-friendly technology, and transparent and competitive billing? The answer to all of these questions is that sales would skyrocket.

Consider, for example, how the power of an improved sales process helped to transform the plodding Deutsche Post. A former state-run monopoly, Deustche Post was privatized in 2000, propelling the German postal workers into brutal competition with global heavyweights such as FedEx and UPS. Open competition served the company well: Employee efficiency soared, as has the company's reputation for providing excellent customer service.

Finally, technology can play a big role in empowering the salesforce. The pharmaceutical industry, for example, has been a pioneer in using product and financial databases to develop sales call strategies and model customer profitability. You may often see pharmaceutical industry sales representatives sitting in their cars in hospital parking lots simulating the optimal product mix to maximize growth and margins in their accounts. By combining laptops, Wi-Fi, cell phones, and Blackberries, the pharmaceutical industry has been able to free up their sales reps to spend more than 95 percent of their working time directly interacting with customers.

7. PRICING STRATEGY AND EXECUTION

Pricing is the most neglected area in business operations and perhaps in management as a whole. A close-up look at the issue of pricing will show how this neglected area can be turned into an important strategic tool that both improves the bottom line and fosters growth.

The fundamental tenet of demand markets is that prices are set by the market, giving consumers the balance of power and leaving companies out in the cold. This is only half true, however. Research reveals that most customers are familiar with fewer than 100 price points. Furthermore, emotional patterns and ties to products tend to be much more influential than previously believed, both in the B2C and B2B market space. The result: Management does, in fact, have power over pricing, and sound strategies and optimization techniques can pay off handsomely.

Pricing measures have significant advantages over classic cost restructuring programs. For example, pricing has direct influence—and generally the highest leverage—on profits. Companies can implement new pricing strategies much more quickly than cost saving programs. Yet, as a highly emotional component of company policy, pricing also carries considerable risk.

Pricing techniques are closely tied to three concepts that hold varying degrees of weight, depending on the industry:

- *(Single) product management* helps companies find introductory price levels of a single product as well as price ceilings of already-introduced products.

- *Customer management* is especially important in service industries and B2B settings. It comprises dynamic and customer-specific price elements that are also known as *yield management*.

- *Assortment management* is related to the choices and pricing of aggregated products and product lines. It determines the optimal assortment complexity and price levels and considers complementary offerings and substitutes.

Pricing tools can, therefore, be assigned to one of three groups: products, customers, and assortment. These three elements describe different tool sets, but because they increase in complexity, they can also be thought of as stages of excellence, evolving from the most simple product management tools into elaborate assortment and product-line management. (For a more in-depth look at how to assess pricing using these concepts, please see the Appendix.)

GRACO

The final case study on the first growth stretch is a company in an undeniably unglamorous industry—fluid-handling equipment and systems. Graco is a Minneapolis-based company that began with the invention of a grease gun for lubricating cars that was powered by air pressure, rather than a hand pump. More than 75 years later, Graco has grown into a US$500 million global company, with three main business units:

- Industrial and automotive, which supplies equipment for painting and applying sealants and adhesives along the assembly line for new car manufacturing.
- Contractor equipment, which provides paint spraying equipment to professional house painters.
- Lubrication equipment, which provides pumps for automotive lubricants, including the equipment used for oil changes at automotive servicing and repair shops.

Graco's flawless execution of its straightforward growth model keeps it head and shoulders above its competitors year after year. Despite tough conditions in all three of its customer segments, Graco has managed to steal share from its competitors. Over the past five years, revenues have grown by 5 percent per year and profits by 12 percent per year. At the same time, it has paid off all of its debt and increased its dividend by more than 55 percent. But the big winners have been its shareholders.

What has allowed Graco to grow where others have not? Graco relies on its core strengths:

- *Value:* Although Graco is a fluid-handling company, it defines its objectives around the needs of its customers, "solving difficult manufacturing problems, increasing productivity, improving quality, conserving energy, saving expensive materials, controlling environmental emissions, and reducing labor costs."[1]

- *Innovation:* Graco continuously strives to improve the performance and quality of its products. In fact, its stated objective is to generate at least 30 percent of each year's sales from products introduced in the past three years. In addition, Graco innovates its business processes. The company recently launched an inventory management system, the Graco EDI system, which allows Graco's distributors to check inventory levels and place orders online.

- *Market coverage:* Graco relentlessly focuses on building market share and market penetration. Again, its goal is to generate at least 5 percent of each year's sales from markets entered in the past three years. Graco tailors its growth strategy around expanding its distribution network and making focused, complementary acquisitions. And Graco enjoys the benefits of being a market share leader. In the contractor business, for example, the company believes it has more than 50 percent market share.

The message from these case studies is clear: Companies that achieve strong growth start by building simple, but solid, growth engines. Their growth models are not fancy or complex, but they reinforce and execute those growth models every day. As a result, the benefits accrue to these companies and their shareholders for years to come.

CHAPTER 8

Organization: Creating High-Performing Companies

Acompany's organizational structure can be a double-edged sword when it comes to growth: It can either cut open a wide path to growth by fostering innovation and creating a frictionless environment in which all processes are aligned with all goals or sever the ability to grow altogether by imbuing an overarching sense of discord. A lack of organizational cohesion typically leads to infighting among divisions, misaligned compensation programs, and slow decision-making processes, all of which, over time, can lead to death by a thousand cuts.

We believe that a company's organizational structure and all of the intangible things that go with it can work together to unlock its growth potential. The key is to identify structural barriers in your company and eliminate them.

Many of the operational growth drivers we explored in the last chapter are relatively quick and straightforward to implement, but developing organizational excellence takes both time and patience.

In this chapter, we discuss organizational best practices and how to replicate them, using case studies that showcase the best—

and sometimes not the best—approaches. To set the stage, we look at Goldman Sachs, the global investment banking powerhouse whose organizational structure and flexibility have allowed it to capitalize on growth opportunities before its competitors could even convene the right decision-makers to decide whether to compete. In other words, it had won the race before its competitors ever heard the starting gun.

GOLDMAN SACHS

At Goldman Sachs, the culture of growth has been embedded in the organization since its inception in 1869. In the ever-changing and dynamic business of investment banking, Goldman Sachs has maintained its preeminence by finding, developing, and dominating the fastest growing and most profitable parts of the business.

Operated for most of its history as a partnership and now completing the transition to a publicly traded company, Goldman Sachs' organizational structure is unique in the way it manages to foster both corporate loyalty and an entrepreneurial spirit among its employees. The result is a positive work environment that continues to produce significant innovations and relentless competitive drive.

The list of innovations and market leadership moves that Goldman Sachs has made over the years is long and impressive. Some of the highlights include:

- Creating and subsequently dominating block trading, in which large blocks of an individual stock are traded among investors.

- Rapidly developing and eventually dominating the M&A advisory and financing business from the late 1980s through the 1990s.

- Reaping huge financial rewards from creating the equity risk arbitrage business (betting on the short-term share price movements of companies targeted for acquisition) in the late 1980s.

■ Dominating the equity initial public offering (IPO) market since the mid-1950s, when it orchestrated the US$560 million Ford Motor Company stock offering, which was the largest-ever public share flotation at the time.

■ Moving into dot-com IPOs and financing during the boom years of the late 1990s.

■ Creating a strong revenue stream by shifting capital and focus into proprietary trading during the economic downturn that began in 2001. This helped Goldman Sachs sustain its profitability throughout the slump, whereas other, less-aggressive competitors have floundered.

Goldman Sachs' strengths are embedded in its culture and modus operandi unlike any other company. Having built an extremely flexible and opportunistic business model and organizational structure, it can reallocate capital and people resources quickly and effectively, which allows it to capitalize on new business opportunities and new geographic markets. For example, in the early 1990s when Asian markets began to show signs of rapid growth and potentially large deals, Goldman Sachs moved in aggressively, hiring and transferring in senior people and opening offices rapidly.

Goldman Sachs also moves faster, more decisively, and with more momentum than its competition. It pulls off deals that initially seem so daunting in their size that competitors don't consider them possible. And when others deem investment too risky, Goldman Sachs finds a way to address the dangers and mitigate them.

How does Goldman Sachs achieve this high-performing organization-driven growth culture? There are three key dimensions. First, Goldman Sachs has a strong, unifying culture, which is best illustrated by excerpts from its 14 business principles:

1. Our clients' interests always come first. Our experience shows that if we serve our clients well, our own success will follow.

2. Our assets are our people, capital and reputation. If any of these is ever diminished, the last is the most difficult to restore.

4. . . . Though we may be involved in a wide variety and heavy volume of activity, we would, if it came to a choice, rather be best than biggest.

5. We stress creativity and imagination in everything we do. While recognizing that the old way may still be the best way, we constantly strive to find a better solution to a client's problems. We pride ourselves in having pioneered many of the practices and techniques that have become standard in the industry.

8. . . . We have found that teamwork often produces the best results. We have no room for those who put their own interests ahead of the interest of the firm and its clients.

11. . . . We constantly strive to anticipate the rapidly changing needs of our clients and to develop new services to meet those needs. We know that the world of finance will not stand still and that complacency can lead to extinction.[1]

Against this cultural backdrop lies the second plank of Goldman Sachs' organization-driven growth model: It hires the best people and motivates them with big financial rewards based on performance. Basically, Goldman Sachs offers talented people the opportunity to "get rich" and advance as quickly as their performance and talent enable them to. As a private partnership, Goldman Sachs was also able to tailor its profit-sharing programs free from the scrutiny of shareholders. And although it is making the transition to a publicly traded company, Goldman Sachs has no desire to fix what isn't broken. In a recent proxy statement, Goldman Sachs describes a new compensation model designed to replicate and tailor the attributes and benefits of a partnership-style profit sharing and compensation program to a publicly traded company.

The third dimension of Goldman Sachs' organizational structure is a relentless focus on improving and optimizing the company's governance and administrative structures. Clearly, setting and managing the boundaries for a business as dynamic and ever changing as Goldman Sach's is a daunting challenge.

Many companies in similar situations opt for rigid structures and decision-making processes that undergo formal reviews at regular intervals, generally annually. But as Goldman Sachs knows, the trees with the most flexibility—those that are able to sway with the wind—are the ones left standing at the end of the day. Thus, rather than imposing a dogmatic system, Goldman Sachs encourages a fluid approach to managing its governance and administrative structures, viewing them as a source of strength and competitive advantage. It is perpetually reviewing and tailoring them to adapt to changing market, economic, and geopolitical conditions. Although it does this at the senior-most levels of the organization, there is broad input from across the company.

True, Goldman Sachs stands out for its uniqueness, but it also offers a number of lessons that companies in any industry can benefit from. A solid organizational structure can generate and sustain a growth-oriented culture that is largely insulated from disruptive external factors. A growth-oriented organizational structure can also reduce, if not entirely remove, barriers to the creativity necessary to develop new innovations in products and services, regardless of the industry. Finally, Goldman Sachs's experience underscores that holding fast to an organizational growth mission does not mean sacrificing flexibility: On the contrary, it means embracing it.

Goldman Sachs illustrates how one of the best companies in the world uses the power of its organizational structure and business processes to capture growth opportunities more effectively than its competitors. And when hit by outside turbulence, this strength quickly transforms into a protective shield. No company is entirely immune to market unrest, but when the investment banking industry has been rocked by various controversies, Goldman Sachs has held steady, usually emerging either unscathed or at least much less affected than its competitors.

But not all companies have growth-oriented organizations like Goldman Sachs. In fact, in almost all of the companies we've worked with, we've seen significant organizational and cultural barriers to growth. These obstacles are typically found at organizational interfaces or are embedded within the organization structure. They also generally relate to decision-making, cultural, or compensation issues. We next look at how senior executives can identify each of these potential barriers and offer suggestions for turning these impediments into opportunities.

ELIMINATE FRICTION

Client after client, year after year, it became increasingly clear to us that organization problems were endemic in every industry in every region. And executives that we've worked with know this; they know that their organizational structure is, in one way or another, impeding growth. But within any given organizational structure, there are many moving parts, and diagnosing which run smoothly and which need improvement requires a closer look.

One of the most common issues we found is that various functional divisions in a company are not coordinated—with the result that they often end up working against one another. A leading European garden tool manufacturer learned firsthand how damaging organizational discord can be. In a focused drive to meet their numbers and seal their deals, the salespeople began reducing prices. Not only were the discounted prices unsustainable, but the capabilities and resources of the other departments, such as distribution, couldn't keep up with the surge in demand. The result was lost revenues and poor delivery service, which, in turn, led to unsatisfied customers.

Discord among the functional groups resonates with companies everywhere, and as this example illustrates, one small—seemingly harmless—turf war can quickly turn into a zero-sum game: In the hunt for short-term or short-sighted wins, long-term growth is sacrificed. To avoid falling into the same traps, there are a few key areas to look at, starting from the top down.

The structure of the board of management and the backgrounds of its members can be telling. Does the company have a sales and marketing team representative on the board? Are controllers or financial analysts predominant?

Another common barrier to growth is a senior leadership team that is effectively isolated from the rest of the company. A European steel and engineering conglomerate with 17 subsidiaries had two layers of management on top of the market-facing companies: one for the entire group and one for four different business units. The result was not only excessive bureaucracy, including higher costs, but also a slower decision-making process. Ultimately, the added time to make critical decisions reduced reaction time and destroyed revenue, particularly for the business units that were in fast-moving markets.

When management is separated from the real workings of the business, miscommunication can become a significant problem. In some cases, there is simply an overabundance of information with the critical pieces getting lost in the din. In other cases, the corporate culture might suppress honest and open communication among the various layers. Intentional or not, the outcome is that the top level never receives a clear picture from the lower levels, where groups of people try to soften hard truths out of fear that top managers adhere to the "shoot the messenger" principle.

Often, long-standing functional structures also become barriers to growth. A leading engineering company, for example, had four strong product lines, but the functional organization among sales, engineering, manufacturing, and operations prevented the product lines from growing. How so? When the sales engineers sold the machines, the design engineers complained that they had sold "the wrong machine at the wrong price—the price was too low." The manufacturing arm of the company then set out to undermine both the sales team and the design engineers, saying and then proving that both had developed a bad machine—"one that did not work at all." Although we are exaggerating the situation to the level of a caricature to make our point, it is a point worth making. Every day, people undermine one another in an effort to get ahead, and in the process, they undermine the organization.

In addition, if such fissures become too deep, they may trigger cultural problems in the company that can be difficult to resolve. One solution may be a charismatic leader who is responsible for a product throughout its process, from development to sales. Unfortunately, the pool of talented people who know the ins and outs of manufacturing as well as sales is small. To break down its structural barriers, the engineering company decided to reorganize its product divisions and lowered product and project costs. For its efforts, the company was rewarded with a significant increase in profits and revenue growth.

Some of the most pernicious organizational issues appear after companies merge. How frequently do acquired companies, for example, stop growing after they lose their independence and became part of a larger entity? As we mentioned, there are not only additional costs associated with multiple layers of management, but also control issues. Added bureaucracy can lead to drawn-out decision-making that, over time, will impede a company's ability to grow. This is particularly true for large *mergers of equals* because there is a great deal of scope for management teams to debate and disagree over, such as who will lead the new company.

The fact that this happens over time is key: Both the merger strategy and postmerger integration plans might have been a complete success, but the organizational roadblocks slowly appear when the larger group begins to impose its culture on the acquired company. Only a handful of companies have been able to consistently integrate new business units without upsetting a strong organizational framework. Cisco is one. The secret? Minimal overhead layers, maximum freedom within a few but very stringent budgetary targets, and fast decision-making processes at the top levels of the company.

BREAK DOWN GROWTH BARRIERS

One of the most common organizational barriers emerges when a company's organizational framework does not mesh with its needs. A matrix organization, for example, does not have a hierarchical reporting structure. People can report to more than one person and more than one business unit. Yet from a cultural standpoint, it is not always strategically necessary or appropriate. Consider the case of a pharmaceutical company that opted for a matrix structure. With no solid reporting hierarchy, its most important product was managed by people who were connected to it only through dotted-line responsibilities. As conflict over functional and regional interests took center stage, the product floundered. When the company adopted a more streamlined, simpler organizational structure with solid-line reporting, revenues shot up by 15 percent.

It's interesting that difficulties with the matrix organization have plagued a number of European pharmaceutical companies, with the same growth-inhibiting effect as in our example. This may explain, at least partly, why European pharmaceutical companies have lost substantial market share to their British and American counterparts.

Consider, too, how a noncompetitive value chain can be an obstacle to an organization. When Japanese automakers invaded the Western market during the 1980s, the American and European producers were mired in deeply integrated supply chains. There was a hierarchy of suppliers and systems suppliers all angling for business and saddling the automakers with cost structures that were 20 percent to 30 percent above the market prices being established by the Japanese. Western automakers were able to regain their footing only after significantly restructuring their operations. They streamlined their core competencies such as design and marketing and outsourced all noncore functions to outside suppliers. In so doing, their cost structures settled in around 25 percent instead of the unwieldy 70 percent, which was the going rate for employing a hierarchy of suppliers and systems providers.

In developing the Endgames Curve, we discovered a strong relationship between the level of consolidation and the depth of economic value added. Indeed, redefining the value chain to concentrate on core competencies can reduce overall costs by 25 percent to 30 percent—with ripple effects on market potential and thus on growth. By definition, core competencies differentiate the company from its key competitors. In recent years, this definition has narrowed. Ask anyone at Nike what the company does, and you will probably hear that it designs and markets sports shoes and gear. Nike does not manufacture shoes and gear; it has neither a salesforce to sell shoes and gear nor a distribution arm to circulate them around the world. Nike creates new products and puts a brand around them. For everything else, it outsources.

Nike and other sports shoe manufacturers were among the first to reduce in-house functions to focus exclusively on design and marketing. By establishing large manufacturing centers first in Thailand and Korea and finally in China, companies were able to produce high-quality shoes at unbeatable prices.

Today, consumer goods companies such as Procter & Gamble, engineering companies such as Alstom, and financial services firms such as Deutsche Bank are taking a page from the sports shoemakers and substantially reducing their in-house functions to focus on their core capabilities. In the process, they are significantly lowering their total costs, increasing their cost competitiveness, and improving their growth potential.

Fortunately for managers, a great deal of research has been conducted on how to create high-performing organizations—in particular, being adept at deploying high-performing cross-functional teams to address specific business issues. General Electric developed a concept called *workout* in which, when a critical business problem is identified, General Electric forms a cross-functional team to address it. Resources are often temporarily reassigned to work full time on these teams until the problem is solved. These teams are also sometimes formed within smaller General Electric lines of business, but other times they are given a very high, companywide profile and mandate. General Electric's success in consolidating its vendors and in reengineering its global supply chain is heavily rooted in its workout concept. This success has not gone unnoticed. A handful of companies have adapted the workout process to suit their own needs. Coca-Cola, for example, is trying to push decision-making authority down to lower levels of its organization. Procter & Gamble has aggressively outsourced many of its noncore business processes, and General Motors has been an innovator in building a flexible organization to better respond to business challenges and opportunities.

The best CEOs put deciding on—and then tailoring—the optimal organizational structure at the top of their agendas. They review their organizational structure regularly, and some have become very innovative in finding and developing new strategies including outsourcing, value chain reconfiguration, and creating utilities. But, as always, implementation is key. As executives at Sara Lee know all too well, even the seemingly best-laid plans often have unexpected wrinkles.

SARA LEE

In the case of Sara Lee, the company captured the imagination of the consumer products industry in 1997 by announcing a *deverticalization* strategy. The core components of the strategy involved outsourcing all of Sara Lee's manufacturing operations to focus on freeing up management attention and cash to pursue and invest in growth opportunities. Specifically, Sara Lee wanted its senior managers to spend more time and financial resources on brand building and beefing up advertising and marketing efforts. In addition, some of the cash freed up through outsourcing went to buy back the company's stock in an effort to lower debt levels and boost the share price.

But the success of the program was undermined by a number of factors, which ultimately reverted management attention back to the distractions they were trying to avoid in the first place. First, the transition to outsourcing the manufacturing plants took longer than expected, and the same Wall Street analysts who initially applauded the outsourcing decision began criticizing the company for its slow progress.

In addition, contamination problems in one of Sara Lee's factories led to a recall of nearly 15 million pounds of meat in late 1998. The plant was temporarily closed. Wall Street analysts wondered aloud how Sara Lee could manage an outsourced manufacturing operation when it had difficulty managing one that it owned and operated.

Five years since the drive for deverticalization was first announced, Sara Lee's business results have been mixed. Its average annual growth rate in revenues for the period 1998 to 2002 was just 1.3 percent, with profits at just 3 percent, well below the industry average. Interestingly, in an environment in which Sara Lee's larger competitors are all rapidly acquiring smaller or weaker players, Sara Lee has just announced another organization-driven growth strategy. Called its "Reshaping Program," the objective is to divest the company of a number of noncore product lines and businesses and refocus the growth of its business on three areas: foods and beverage, intimates and underwear, and household products. Although it is difficult to predict how this new strategy will play out over the long term, Sara Lee's share price declined sharply in late 2002, into mid-2003.

IMPROVE DECISION-MAKING PROCESSES

Ensuring that efficient decision-making processes are in place is particularly important. Business historians will no doubt recall a CEO by the name of Harold Geneen, the legendary leader of ITT during the 1960s and 1970s. At the time, ITT was one of the largest conglomerates in the United States, with businesses in several hundred different industries. Despite this massive portfolio, Geneen believed that he and he alone was empowered to make major business decisions. He spent the vast majority of his time in business review meetings and ran the company successfully for nearly two decades. When he retired, however, the company experienced major problems because all of the company's decision-making processes revolved around one position in the organization, and no one could possibly run the company the way Harold Geneen had run it.

Although ITT may be an extreme example, all too often we see companies falling into the consensus trap, in which all major decisions require the full agreement of top management, particularly during crises or other turbulent periods. Indeed, consensus-based decision-making, which is a benefit in the times of *beginning growth*, best illustrated in the Japanese economic wonder following World War II, becomes a liability in times of restructuring when the company moves toward *adjusting growth*. As companies are forced to adjust to turbulent or volatile times, consensus building becomes a barrier: Trying to get everyone to agree to a decision means the company is unable to react quickly to short-term events. The result is that no unpopular decision is made, or in some cases, no decision is made at all. The obvious downside is that not all good decisions are popular. Turbulent times require organizational structures that allow for—and encourage—fast and final decision-making.

Decision-making processes can be a growth enabler. From an opportunistic standpoint, Jack Welch was legendary for being able to convene his board of directors within one or two hours to make a decision on a potential acquisition. Such organizational speed can be a competitive advantage and allow companies to take advantage of growth opportunities and propositions before competitors can blink. In a more steady-state environment, smooth, well thought-through decision processes ensure that managers at the right level of an organization are making the right day-to-day decisions that promote growth initiatives.

ALIGN COMPENSATION AND GROWTH

Closely connected to the organizational structures is the compensation system, which helps promote and sustain a positive work environment. Those positions or departments that garner the most attention will likely receive the biggest budget. But how is this executed? Do the biggest rewards go to those who meet the company's functional interests—for example, those who help the company achieve the lowest cost per piece and the highest quality? Or are the rewards saved for those who meet or exceed sales or profit volume in a specific region? What about compensation for those who meet or exceed product sales targets or come up with the greatest technological improvements to a process? Shouldn't there be a reward for spectacular innovation?

For example, the CEO of an industrial products company had garnered a 60 percent market share. Because he was nearing retirement, he resisted his board's desire to aggressively pursue new growth initiatives because he was afraid to put his core business at risk and because he knew he could coast for another two or three years until his retirement with the same business model. The underlying issue was that his compensation package did not reinforce the board's growth ambitions, because he was not motivated to change.

Finding the right balance between these conflicting elements is key, but both our findings and experience show that imbalances are far too common. Consider the European subsidiary of a global food company that was unable to successfully market an American product line in Europe. Despite the failure, the COO was rewarded for cutting costs. No one mentioned (though everyone noticed) his failure to increase overall revenue, which hurt the overall success of the European organization.

To summarize the key messages from this chapter and to reinforce the key message that a company's organization structure and processes should be a growth enabler, not a hinderer, we look at another case study of a global banking industry leader.

HSBC HOLDINGS

HSBC Holdings, the world's second largest bank, is another example of how organization structure and culture can lead to the successful creation of growth and profitability. The bank, founded in Hong Kong in 1865 by a Scotsman named Thomas Sutherland, has been operated by the same growth principles of discipline, patience, and thrift since its inception. In fact, as Figure 8.1 shows, the company cites "HSBC Character" as the cornerstone of its growth strategy.

For many years, HSBC was a small bank operating in Asia. Its lending business was extremely profitable, particularly in Hong Kong, and by the 1980s, management began to develop global aspirations. HSBC always operated on a long-term time frame, and the bank waited patiently for the right time to make acquisitions to buy its way into major global markets. In 1980, it bought a controlling stake in the Marine Midland Bank in the United States, and in 1987, it began a five-year process (which involved shifting its corporate headquarters from Hong Kong to London) to acquire Midland Bank in the United Kingdom. In 2000, it acquired Credit Commercial de France (CCF), one of France's largest banks. It has supplemented these major acquisitions with tens of

FIGURE 8.1   HSBC'S ORGANIZATION-DRIVEN
             GROWTH MODEL

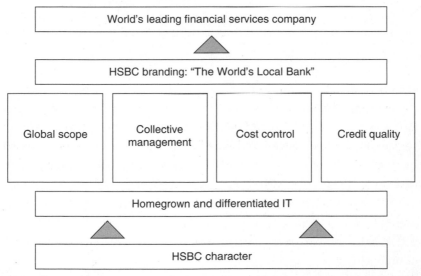

Source: HSBC Holdings presentation to the Banc of America Securities Conference, September 2002.

smaller deals to build up its global banking presence, particularly in non-OECD countries, and to add scale to its fund management, leasing, investment banking, insurance, and other businesses.

Because of its Asian beginnings, HSBC has such depth of international experience embedded in its organization that it can spot when a country has fallen on hard times and when attractive acquisition prices may follow. The international experience also allows HSBC to be comfortable pursuing growth opportunities that other banks may view as too risky. China and India are two such markets, where HSBC is adopting a bet-the-farm mentality, while competitors are approaching the markets more cautiously and adopting a wait-and-see approach. HSBC's international institutional knowledge and contact list sometimes allow HSBC to help shape the policy of emerging market governments and regulators on the development of the financial services industry that is beneficial to HSBC's long-term competitive position.

The international nature of HSBC's organization is viewed by the bank as one of its biggest sources of current and future growth. The bank is an entrenched, major competitor in 81 countries globally, with 30 million retail customers, 2 million small-to-medium enterprise (SME) customers, and 1,200 corporate multinational customers. The bank has systematic and rigorous business processes in place to identify, transfer, and share best practices in acquiring customers and reducing costs. The bank concentrates mainly on organic growth, primarily by leveraging its international network and by adopting a customer-driven marketing approach organized around customer needs and business segments. When it acquires businesses, it identifies targets based on their ability to extend HSBC's global reach or to contribute revenue synergies to HSBC's existing businesses.

Culturally, HSBC has a tendency to be thrifty and cautious, which when embedded within HSBC serves its growth strategy as well. This facet of the culture led HSBC to avoid pumping up growth in the 1990s through expensive acquisitions. At the time, branded as "dull," "old-fashioned," and "boring" for not emulating rivals such as Credit Suisse First Boston, J.P. Morgan Chase, and Citigroup by acquiring an investment bank, HSBC is now avoiding their postbubble troubles of insider-trading scandals, SEC investigations, bad loans, and high-cost structures. As Sir John Bond, HSBC's chairman says, "We are cautious about businesses that rely too much on individuals. They lead to ever-increasing demands for their people that they need [to be paid] more of the profits." As the *Wall Street Journal* put it in an article from October 18, 2002, "the dull but probe-free and steadily profitable conservatism of HSBC looks pretty good [right now]."

HSBC also invests heavily in the training of its people and, in so doing, reinforces its growth culture. The training courses teach employees how to leverage HSBC's global footprint, how to identify and address customer needs, and how to focus on profitable businesses. As a result, HSBC avoids popular industry practices such as the loss-leading practice of discounting loan rates or making potentially unprofitable loans to companies in the hope of winning lucrative investment-banking fees. HSBC's loan write-offs and provisions are almost always lower than its major competitors.

The bank also positions its independence vis-à-vis its customers by force-ranking companies rated by its equity analysts within a given industry and by banning "hold" recommendations that are really a code word for a "sell" recommendation. This eliminates a publicly perceived conflict of interest, which sees equity analysts as biased toward higher-than-warranted ratings on stocks to position their affiliated investment banking business favorably for corporate advisory work.

The HSBC organization-driven growth model is not an exciting one. But by sticking to its growth strategy, leveraging its institutional experience, and exploiting its advantages, HSBC has created a lasting organic growth engine that produces value and results.

These case studies illustrate how growth models are reinforced and strengthened through the second growth step—the organizational step. In the first step, we saw how companies can build the minimum operational baseline for growth. In this chapter, we've seen how leading companies have used the critical components of their organization to embed their growth model and strategy into every facet of their business. They translate amorphous organizational concepts such as culture, globalization, governance, and administrative structures into lasting, enduring competitive advantage. In contrast, other companies sometimes take shortcuts or turn to quick-fix solutions and often end up with mixed results.

In the next chapter, we turn to strategy, the third step, as the next crucial building block of a company's high-performing growth model.

CHAPTER 9

Strategy: Exploiting
Strategic Levers

S o far in this part, we have discussed how operations and organization can affect growth. The operations dimension provides companies with a relatively quick, low-risk growth boost; the organization dimension, although more difficult to implement, establishes an enduring platform for growth. Only after a company has mastered these two steps should it turn to strategy. Without the infrastructure that operations and organization create, even the most well-developed strategy will likely fail. Indeed, the list of companies that have won in the marketplace on strategy alone is short at best.

Yet, when a company has done its work and laid a solid foundation, using strategy as a growth lever can propel a company upward within the ranks of its industry and help keep it there. Toyota, for example, patiently pursued its strategy for decades before emerging as a leader in the automotive industry. It also invented and pioneered the most popular management techniques in the industry, while at the same time resisting value-destroying management fads.

TOYOTA

The adage "Slow and steady wins the race" seems to epitomize Toyota's strategy, which for decades has been centered on slow, deliberate geographic expansion. But don't be fooled by the apparent simplicity of its plan. Few companies have demonstrated Toyota's foresight, tenacity, and shrewdness in moving from being a local player to a world leader. And it has taken every step in full view of its competitors.

Toyota's geographic expansion began with exporting cars from its Japanese assembly plants to the United States. It followed this move by increasing its Asian infrastructure throughout the 1970s and into the 1990s, creating strong dealer and parts networks across Hong Kong, Taiwan, the Philippines, and Southeast Asia.

By leveraging the economies of scale generated by its huge Japanese plants, Toyota expanded on its Asian manufacturing footprint, employing completely knocked down (CKD) assembly plants, which are essentially finishing plants. Toyota continued to export engines, transmissions, and chassis built in Japan to various local markets. When the timing was right, Toyota turned its attention further abroad: During the 1980s, it began building assembly plants and supplier infrastructures in the United States. It then established an assembly plant in Australia, designed as a springboard to bolster its market growth in Southeast Asia and the Middle East. Finally, it took the European market by storm by building massive manufacturing plants in the United Kingdom in 1992 and in France in 2000.

Now, ranked as the third-largest automaker in the world, Toyota dominates Japan as well as smaller Asian and Middle Eastern markets and is among the leaders in the remaining major North American and European markets. But Toyota is far from finished, and it has already mapped out its next moves—setting its sights on the high-growth opportunities in China and India.

Toyota also pioneered a number of management techniques and principles that continue to stand the test of time in the automotive industry. It recognized early on, for example, that the relationship with parts suppliers is a double-edged sword: Building tight relationships, fostering open communication, and being able to exert control is good for business, but owning parts suppliers is expensive. GM, Ford, and German automakers have suffered the burdens of high labor costs from their parts business for years; only recently have Ford and GM spun off Visteon and Delphi, their long-time parts units.

Toyota, meanwhile, adopted a different approach. It maintains small but significant equity stakes and management positions in its parts suppliers' organizations but still maintains an arm's-length ownership position. In the late 1980s and early 1990s in Southeast Asia, for example, Toyota negotiated and capitalized on a complex automotive free-trade agreement (the BBC agreement) to set up a huge low-cost parts manufacturing network over which Toyota maintained tight operating and management control but held little of the ownership risk. This low-cost parts network allowed Toyota to make cars for less cost and steal or build share at the expense of its competitors.

Toyota has always been a pioneer in its assembly and product design as well. It pioneered the manufacturing concept of lean manufacturing, which has been emulated by all competitors and is applied to manufacturing operations in other industries. It resisted the design practices of its competitors by refusing to proliferate brands. Instead, it has gone to market with basically the same model line-up for years. The Toyota Corolla, for example, is known the world over as the leading small car.

Toyota has always focused on customer needs as a cornerstone for its growth strategy. It pioneered the idea of limiting options packages, thus avoiding proliferating design combinations that slow down the ordering process, and raised customers' expectations for what they would get if they bought a Toyota. In addition, Toyota has always paid close attention to its dealer network, investing heavily in extensive training and dealership management programs. As a result, Toyota dealerships are managed to the same standards around the world, in contrast to many of its competitors. Finally, Toyota has always been responsive to changes in its customer preferences. It was the first automotive company to single out the environment as a plank in its strategy. Coming out of that initiative is the Prius, the world's first mass-marketed hybrid electric power and gasoline car.

Whereas in other industries strategic portfolio moves can be important, in the automotive industry Toyota has not followed its competitors by diversifying into new businesses. While competitors dabbled in extracurricular activities—General Motors diversified into computer services and electronics; Ford, in financial services, dot-com ventures, and buy-outs of its dealers; and Chrysler, in aerospace—Toyota has consistently stuck to its knitting and remained focused on the automotive business. Toyota simply watched as other automakers gobbled each other up in recent years:

- GM acquired Daewoo, as well as significant equity stakes in Fiat, Suzuki, Subaru, and Isuzu.
- Ford acquired Volvo, Rover, Mazda, and Jaguar.
- DaimlerBenz acquired Chrysler and Mitsubishi.
- Renault acquired Nissan.

Bucking the M&A (mergers and acquisitions) trend, Toyota has gained market share (and in so doing, has de facto consolidated the industry) by growing organically and by forcing its competitors to shrink, be acquired, or go out of business.

The results achieved by Toyota's growth strategy have been outstanding. Toyota is the third largest auto producer in the world. It has the highest market capitalization, highest revenue and profitability growth rates, and cleanest balance sheet of any competitor in the industry. It has the number-one selling product in the U.S. market (the Camry) and is consistently rated by customers as having the best quality, service, and value in a car purchase (see Figure 9.1).

While not glamorous, its strategy for growth has required discipline and conviction to carry it out successfully. The results speak for themselves. Any company can learn from Toyota's management strategy for growth.

FIGURE 9.1   TOYOTA LEADS THE AUTOMOTIVE INDUSTRY

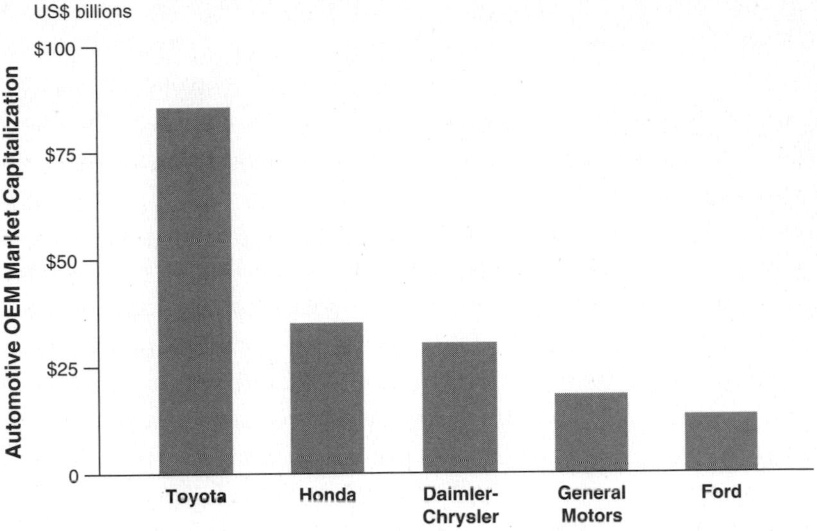

Source: www.finance.yahoo.com; March 27, 2003.

Companies that successfully use strategy as a growth enabler do so by knowing their core competency—the one thing they do better than anyone else—and leverage it for maximum benefit. Toyota, for example, makes good cars at a reasonable price. It has used that competency to grow its business globally and dominate all major vehicle segments. In the remainder of this chapter, we examine the dimensions of a successful growth strategy and discuss how they can be used as catalysts to grow your company's business.

WHAT INDUSTRY ARE YOU REALLY IN?

Before using strategy as a growth enabler, it is necessary to understand what business and industry your company is really competing in. It sounds simple, doesn't it? But there are many misnomers whirling around about what industry a company truly competes in. For example, GM is often viewed as a car company, but it is really in a number of industries, including passenger cars, trucks, automotive parts, and service and financial services, each of which has its own set of competitors and strategic dynamics. IBM isn't just a computer hardware company; it also competes in the software and consulting services industries. Citigroup isn't simply a financial services company; it competes in the retail banking, commercial banking, brokerage, investment banking, leasing, and insurance industries.

The Value-Building Growth Matrix discussed earlier is an excellent starting point to gain a true understanding of your business and industry. It forces a company to confront its historic business performance and to realistically assess itself against competitors.

Once the industry is defined and competitors that your company competes against are understood, you are in a position to set strategic growth objectives for each business in your portfolio. You are also ready to build an overarching portfolio-wide growth objective. General Electric became famous for its overarching strategic growth objective: to become first or second in global market share in whatever industry it competed. General Electric rationalized—and optimized—its entire business portfolio, aggressively promoting and growing each business until it became a clear leader in its industry. If General Electric did not lead in an industry, it got out of the business.

For companies that do not have the size and scale of General Electric, it is critical to set strategic growth objectives for each part of your business. You have to determine the one thing your company does well that can be leveraged. How can your company become what Toyota is to high-quality cars, what HSBC is to global commercial banking, and what Nestlé is to consumer products? The answer will form the basis of your growth strategy.

WHAT IS YOUR CUSTOMER GROWTH STRATEGY?

Pareto's rule states that 80 percent of a company's business is generated from 20 percent of its customers. It follows, then, that 20 percent of customers contribute to 80 percent of a company's growth, as well. Thus, the starting point for growth should be your best, strongest, and most loyal customers.

Again, many companies build their growth strategy around dominating their best customers. The pharmaceutical giants are well known for developing intricate models of customer buying behavior. These models help them plan which products to sell to which customers and to assess product penetration rates by customer and geographic market. This allows sales representatives to plan their sales calls around optimizing the sales growth and margin potential of each customer.

Similarly, car companies plan their product portfolios around the life cycle of their customers. Smaller cars, such as the Ford Escort or Toyota Corolla, are designed and priced to capture young customers. Station wagons and vans are designed for roominess and to appeal to families, sports cars are for after the siege (when the children have moved out of the house), and larger sedans are for the later years when comfort matters most.

Examine your customer base and try to think through the range of needs of your customers. How can you maximize the value you provide them? How can you provide differentiated services to your best customers? How can you expand your customer base? These are the key questions around which a solid customer growth strategy should be built.

WHAT DISTRIBUTION CHANNELS FUEL THE BEST GROWTH?

Distribution channels are central to a solid growth strategy. When talking about distribution channels with our clients, two strategies usually emerge. A company can dominate either a single distribution channel or multiple distribution channels that serve the same customer base. In a recent assignment, for example, we helped the European market leader in film processing shift its channel strategy. Rather than processing film solely in one channel—retail stores—it moved to the multichannels of the future, processing film in discount drugstores and large-scale retailers. Although these new channels have tighter margins, the volume of processing more than compensates for the lost revenues. As the company's profits and growth rate continue to soar, so does its scale.

For some companies, a single channel strategy is the winning path to growth. But in these situations, it is critical to choose the right distribution channel and strategy. Loblaw's, as we saw earlier, is highly successful at using a single channel—its grocery stores—to push as many products and services as possible to its customers.

WHICH COUNTRIES SHOULD YOU COMPETE IN?

The fourth dimension of a growth strategy calls for optimizing the portfolio of countries your company competes in. Is there a right mix of countries? Does the company have the right emphasis or the right combination of countries for growth, risk, and stability?

The choice is often not obvious. Consider, for example, the German-based market leader in medical supplies. The company was fine as long as it focused on its traditional close-to-home markets: Switzerland, Austria, Scandinavia, and the United Kingdom. Moving into the United States, however, proved problematic. At first, it seemed like a logical next step: The United States represented the company's largest potential market. But although the U.S. market soon accounted for 35 percent of the company's profits, it required 60 percent of its resources.

An evaluation of existing and potential markets revealed that the growth and profit potential in its neighboring European markets was much higher than in the United States. France, Italy, and Spain all offered large, untapped markets with good margins and fewer obstacles (pressure from local competitors, for example).

Many well-known companies have deliberately emphasized or avoided specific country markets. HSBC, for example, has only a small presence in the United States despite being one of the largest banks in the world. The reason, according to HSBC, is that the price of acquisitions is too high in the United States, and it can find better growth opportunities for less money elsewhere. Similarly, GE Capital is notorious for entering depressed markets. It entered Japan in the late 1990s after Japan had endured more than half a decade of recession. General Electric entered Eastern Europe when every other financial institution was leaving due to huge losses, and it entered Southeast Asia following the Asian crisis in 1997 and 1998.

On the other hand, how many companies have blindly plowed money into China despite overwhelming research and data that shows that companies rarely make money there? Making the right choice of countries is a critical component of a company's growth strategy.

WHAT IS THE BEST PRODUCT PORTFOLIO?

Reshaping the product portfolio can significantly improve a company's growth potential. A south European supplier of metal parts in the white goods industry learned this lesson. The company's product portfolio was burdened by six different product groups, each with a different growth and profit profile. To improve its strategic positioning, the company eliminated half of the portfolio and redirected much of its resources and programs to two of the remaining products, while putting the last one on hold. This move, along with several other initiatives, helped the company earn a 40 percent boost in revenues and a 50 percent increase in margins.

When a leader in dental supplies refocused its product portfolio, it saw a 15 percent rise in revenues and 30 percent increase in profits. The supplier's main product portfolio revolved around the chemicals used to produce dentures and fillings. When the company branched out, developing dental anesthetics as well as its core chemicals, it earned mixed success. So the supplier sold its line of dental anesthetics to a specialized pharmaceutical supplier and refocused its product development and sales and marketing teams on its core products. The rewards followed.

Developing strategies around product portfolios requires sound decision-making and good judgment. Several single-product companies have been extremely successful: Coca-Cola, WD-40, and Wrigley are excellent examples. But these companies are fairly unusual. For the majority of companies, success calls for developing a product line along some dimension that can be leveraged, such as technology, functionality, or a bundle of related products. To illustrate this point, we look at a successful implementation of a product-based growth strategy at Teleflex.

TELEFLEX

Teleflex is a diversified electromechanical products company based in Pennsylvania. The company's growth strategy has been domino-like. Teleflex creates and dominates a series of adjacent businesses, all of which are built around its commercial, aerospace, and medical products business units.

Teleflex began as a cable manufacturer, supplying cable for military aircraft to customers such as the British Royal Air Force. Over the years, it has used its expertise in aircraft cable technology to expand into adjacent businesses: providing cable to automotive, marine, and the medical equipment industries. Teleflex also moved beyond aircraft cables to other aircraft applications: producing onboard cargo systems, turbine engine parts, and aerospace electronic technology. Although on the surface Teleflex appears to be a diversified conglomerate, its businesses are strongly interrelated—they all use common products and technologies.

Through acquisitions, Teleflex augments its core growth strategy. The company typically makes several small acquisitions a year. Each deal focuses on bringing in new adjacent technology capabilities or reinforcing Teleflex's existing market position.

Each acquisition is generally integrated into Teleflex's core operations quickly, efficiently, and seamlessly. And growth often begets growth. Several complementary growth benefits arise from Teleflex's strategy:

- Because the business is built on smaller niche applications within big industries, Teleflex must have extremely strong focus on customer needs, requirements, and relationships to spot how the niches evolve. Part of its unifying growth strategy is a focus on solving customer problems with proprietary, innovative products that are not easily replicated by bigger competitors.

- By narrowly defining the areas in which Teleflex competes, the company can build small niches that it can dominate and thereby produce superior returns. As Harold Zuber, Teleflex's chief financial officer, explains, "While we don't have a policy of being number one in our markets, we understand the attractiveness [of being so]."

- In the company's operating objectives and values, many references are made to employee autonomy and empowerment as a source of innovation and risk-taking. These include encouraging autonomous operating units to focus on customer needs; to empower employees through training, education, and trust; and to embrace a management style of "respect for the individual" and "operational autonomy—remote trust." Because of its underlying technology, Teleflex can loosen the grip on its disparate business units to search for growth opportunities more aggressively than its competition.

- The evolution of Teleflex's business into three broad industry segments has implicitly diversified its risk profile because the segments are largely countercyclical. In the early 1990s, for example, growth in its medical business segment was booming while growth in its industrial and aerospace segments was more modest. In the late 1990s, aerospace took off while medical slowed down. These days, Teleflex's industrial segment is growing quickly to make up for slower growth in aerospace.

The results of this growth strategy have been impressive. Teleflex has had 28 consecutive years of increased sales and more than two decades of uninterrupted earnings growth. In an industry characterized by slow growth and low margins, Teleflex's revenue growth over the past five years has averaged 13 percent, and its earnings growth rate has averaged just over 12 percent. Over the past decade, its return on shareholders' equity has averaged more than 15 percent.

WHERE DO MERGERS AND ACQUISITIONS FIT IN?

Mergers, acquisitions, and divestitures all play an important role in the successful realization of the stretch growth strategy. Too often, we see companies that rely exclusively on M&A-driven growth—and as a result they become "one-trick wonders." Although companies such as WorldCom, NCNB, Ahold, Tyco, and AOL Time Warner all began their acquisition sprees with good intentions, they became overreliant on this strategic lever to produce growth. They were forced to chase bigger and bigger deals and ultimately either did one deal too many or one deal too big, and their M&A-driven growth model resulted in massive integration problems and write-offs.

As shown in Figure 9.2, when a company uses M&As to boost growth, patience and thorough analysis are heavily rewarded. The success of most mergers is made or broken in two critical phases: (1) selecting the right acquisition candidate and the right price to pay and (2) quickly and thoroughly integrating the acquired company once the deal is done. Failed M&A strategies usually result from overpaying, choosing the wrong candidate, or being too patient or not ruthless enough during the integration process.

FIGURE 9.2 TWO TYPES OF M&A STRATEGY DOMINATE
FINANCIAL SERVICES CONSOLIDATION TRENDS

"Acquisitions" by
global consolidators

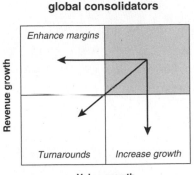

"Mergers" of
equals

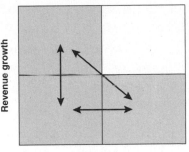

Examples:
- NationsBank/Bank of America
- DBS/Krung Thai Bank
- HSBC/Household International

Examples:
- LB Kiel/Hamburgische Landesbank
- J.P. Morgan/Chase
- BankOne/First Chicago

Source: A.T. Kearney.

Examples that seem almost comical on paper happen all
the time:

- In one company, eight years after a merger, employees still
identify one another as "PMXs" and "PMYs"—people who were
from company X before their merger and people who were
from company Y.

- Companies that pay as much as 70 percent or more of the
price recommended by their advisors just to make sure they
win the deal.

- Acquiring a company in an adjacent industry solely on the
basis of its cross-selling opportunity.

The reality of an M&A strategy is that the most successful acquisitions are just that: acquisitions. Mergers, particularly of two
weaker-performing players, rarely create revenue growth or shareholder value. As Figure 9.2 illustrates, the most successful acquirers

typically buy from a position of strength (upper-right quadrant of the Value-Building Growth Matrix) and purchase companies in the following priorities:

- Turnaround candidates (bottom-left quadrant).

- Margin enhancement candidates, in which the combined entity is able to produce greater economies of scale, thus improving profitability (top-left quadrant).

- Candidates that need new sources of revenue growth (bottom-right quadrant).

- Companies such as GE Capital, NCNB (then Nations-Bank), and HSBC are particularly good at executing this type of acquisition strategy.

In contrast, mergers of equals—mergers of two companies not usually in the top right-hand corner of the matrix—face a much greater challenge in becoming successful. The steep hurdles they face in meshing boards of directors, CEOs and senior management teams, operations, IT systems, and cultures often consume the deal. Recent examples include DaimlerBenz and Chrysler, Royal Insurance and Sun Alliance, J.P. Morgan and Chase, and AOL and Time Warner.

So although acquisitions often offer a quick fix to growth, they make the most sense when they supplement a thorough and comprehensive organic growth strategy.

Now we look at the strategies and results of one of the world's most successful winery businesses, Robert Mondavi. It is an example of a visionary and inspirational growth strategy that was followed through with precision implementation and should serve as a model for any company that aspires to top-notch growth rates.

ROBERT MONDAVI

The stretch growth strategy of the Robert Mondavi Winery is radically different in its approach, but similar in its result. The company's growth strategy was built by a single entrepreneur, Robert G. Mondavi, whose vision was to create a world-class wine industry in California's Napa Valley. Since he and his son, Michael, founded the company in 1966, Robert Mondavi has used several of the strategy-growth dimensions—product innovation, customer segmentation, geographic expansion, and M&A—to become one of the wine industry's global leaders.

When Robert Mondavi Winery was first formed, the Napa Valley was primarily farmland. The grapes grown there were primarily for eating, exported to Midwestern cities. At the time, California's few wine producers were viewed as second or third rate in terms of quality and prestige. French wine producers were the strongest and highest quality wine producers in the world. Besides, American consumers were not accustomed to drinking wine, preferring beer and hard liquor.

Working first in his father's grape distribution business and later in his small winery, Robert Mondavi became increasingly optimistic about the potential for the wine industry in the Napa Valley. After a lengthy trip to the leading wineries in France and a great deal of thought and research on the tastes and preferences of American consumers, he decided to launch the Robert Mondavi Winery.

His first years were dedicated to two growth objectives: getting U.S. consumers to embrace wine as a worthy beverage and producing a globally competitive product. To encourage consumer acceptance, he developed several innovative ideas that have transformed the global industry:

- Mondavi linked the development of the wine industry with the development of the tourism industry, by positioning the Napa Valley's wineries as a tourist destination. He opened a gourmet restaurant and built a food center and a wine tasting room, encouraging people to learn about and taste gourmet foods and wines.

- He redesigned wine products to better suit the American palate, beginning with the introduction of a white wine called

Fumé Blanc, which was sweeter than the popular French Sauvignon Blanc.

▪ He put California wines on the map internationally and achieved his first success in 1972, when the *Los Angeles Times* selected Robert Mondavi Winery's Cabernet Sauvignon as its top red wine of the year. This success continued as Mondavi won several international competitions, much to the dismay and astonishment of French producers.

▪ He focused resources on ensuring the highest levels of product quality and was one of the first winemakers to practice natural farming and to produce products without additives.

Robert Mondavi Winery's success continued, and Robert Mondavi continued to grow his business on the strength of these initial strategies. In the area of tourism, Mondavi promoted the Napa Valley continuously, encouraging top chefs, innkeepers, and restaurateurs to set up shop there. The region has become a huge tourist destination and has spawned similar levels of tourism in the nearby areas of the Sonoma Valley and the Russian River Valley.

On the product front, Mondavi's products rapidly gained popularity as wine was first accepted, and then embraced, by American consumers. Mondavi pioneered the segmentation of consumers by taste and price, using his recently acquired Woodbridge Winery to mass-produce less-pricey wines for the masses while producing wines under his own label for his more discerning wine consumers.

Robert Mondavi Winery invests heavily in consumer research and taste preferences and has continued to purchase California wineries to flesh out its product portfolio by price point, acquiring a host of wineries including the Byron Vineyard & Winery and the Arrowood Vineyards & Winery. He also redesigned his bottles, inventing the popular flange-top bottle, which eliminates the need for a metal capsule over the opening of the bottle. Finally, he built a sophisticated and talented marketing organization that built the Mondavi brands into marketing powerhouses and created brand power within the wine wholesaling and distribution channels.

Mondavi believed that he could spur the growth of the high-end wine market in the United States if he could produce wines that were recognized by wine critics as the best in the world. Mondavi encouraged (and educated) wine critics to spend time with him in the Napa Valley, and in so doing, almost single-handedly created a spin-off industry related to wine reviews and publications including the *Wine Spectator*. Joint ventures and alliances with the leading wineries of the world were part of the Mondavi strategy. The most important, a joint venture with Chateau Mouton Rothschild (France), produced one of the most highly acclaimed wines in the world, Opus One. He also formed joint ventures with the Frescobaldi wineries in Italy, the Errazuriz winery in Chile, and Rosemont Estates in Australia to produce wines from each country in the super-premium segment.

In recent years, the scale of the global wine industry has increased dramatically. Megamergers and cross-border alliances are commonplace. Although the industry remains extremely fragmented, industry powerhouses are beginning to emerge and stake their claims. Robert Mondavi Winery is currently the world's ninth largest winery behind E.&J. Gallo (United States), Foster's Group (Australia), Constellation Brands (United States), and Southcorp (Australia).

Yet, the popularity of wine, especially in the higher-priced segments, may have caused the industry to get ahead of itself. Surplus capacity and overly high prices currently prevail, and many expect a shakeout to occur. Mondavi, with its conservative financial structure and strong heritage of growth, seems to be in a good position to take a leadership position.

On the surface, the Mondavi growth strategy and the Toyota strategy do not seem to have much in common. But, in fact, the similarities are striking. Each company pursued growth through slow but deliberate geographic expansion, high-quality products, detailed consumer research, and attention to consumer needs and preferences. Both also relied on innovative bold approaches to doing business that went against conventional management wisdom in the industry.

Although the three companies profiled in this chapter have very different histories, the lessons learned are consistent: Strategy can be a big differentiator in achieving growth in your company. Each company based its strategy on serving customer needs, putting in place and executing long-term sources of growth, innovative ideas, and risk-taking. All are cornerstones of building strong, robust organic growth engines in a company. Although Toyota, Teleflex, and Robert Mondavi Winery are not in the same business, they have all achieved the same business results: strong enduring track records of profitable growth.

In the next chapter, we look at the final growth step. Companies that reach this level are world-class business leaders. There are not many that can claim this territory, but, again, the lessons learned from the journey can be insightful.

CHAPTER 10

Stretch: Achieving Extraordinary Growth

With everything else in place, it's time to reach for the top by taking a good, long stretch. We call the final step in our growth model *stretch* because if a company takes the journey through the first three growth phases, it should be in peak condition. To move higher, a company must break through several business barriers at once, creating a convergence of operational, organizational, and strategic synergies. In other words, to achieve stretch growth, a company must be firing on all growth cylinders. As the Loblaw's example in Chapter 6 illustrates, this is not easy to do, but the rewards are simply too great not to try.

In this chapter, we take a somewhat different approach to illustrating the stretch growth concept. Because of the complex nature of stretch growth and the need for synergies, we use numerous case studies to illustrate our thinking. We begin by looking at a flagship of this concept: Nestlé.

Nestlé

The core of Nestlé's portfolio of businesses was formed in the late 1800s, beginning with Henri Nestlé's discovery of an alternative substitute for baby's milk. During the same time period, Nestlé's neighbor, Daniel Peter, discovered how to mix milk and cocoa powder to make chocolate milk. The two businesses merged and Nestlé was formed.

One of the hallmarks of Nestlé's growth strategy has been its ability to identify and enter into promising new market segments. Its entry into the coffee market with its flagship product, Nescafé, during World War II is a good example. Nescafé was a hit with American servicemen—with sales almost tripling over the course of the war—and helped turn Nestlé into a large global business.

In the 1980s, Nestlé further expanded its global market presence by building up its presence in Asia, Africa, and the Middle East. It developed a tailored strategy for each country, which included everything from creating a regional brand campaign and reconfiguring product suites to altering package and serving sizes to suit local tastes and preferences.

Toward the early 1990s, Nestlé's top managers began to see potential for consolidation within several of the company's industries. The Berlin Wall had fallen and the doors to Eastern Europe were opening. A number of governments began to relax trade restrictions and foreign ownership limitations. China, for example, began to encourage foreign direct investment. Nestlé saw all of these developments as signs that a round of consolidation would lead to a shake-out in the global food business, so the company went on the offensive, beginning with several large acquisitions in the bottled water and pet food businesses. In many cases, Nestlé's brand and business portfolios were rounded out by its acquisition strategy, particularly in mature industries where two or three acquisitions allowed it to become the dominant player (see Figure 10.1).

Despite its success over the years, Nestlé has been brushed by controversy. In the late 1970s and early 1980s, the company

FIGURE 10.1   NESTLÉ'S GROWTH PORTFOLIO

Nestlé SA		
Product line	**Major brands**	**Notable acquisitions**
Pharmaceutical and cosmetics	L'Oreal	Alcon, equity stake in L'Oreal
Baby foods	Numerous	
Breakfast cereals	Numerous	Joint venture with General Mills
Chocolate and confectionery	Kit Kat, Smarties, Nestlé Crunch	Carnation
Ice cream	Nestlé brands	Dreyer's
Prepared foods	Maggi, Buitoni	Buitoni, Chef America, Stouffer's
Food service	Nestlé	
Beverages	Milo, Nesquik, Nescafé, Nestea	Joint venture with Coca-Cola
Bottled water	Perrier, San Pellegrino	Perrier, San Pellegrino
Petcare	Friskies, Purina	Carnation, Ralston Purina, Spillers

Source: www.nestle.com, A.T. Kearney analysis.

endured significant product boycotts over its marketing practices of infant formula products in third-world countries. These boycotts severely damaged the company's reputation. Management ultimately addressed the issues and, in many respects, emerged a stronger company. Today, Nestlé openly communicates and shares its corporate business principles. It outlines its business practices and policies on human rights, infant health and nutrition, the environment, child labor, supplier relationships, and other issues related to compliance and ethics.

Nestlé's organization structure and culture are also very powerful and help set it further apart from the pack. As a matrix organization, Nestlé remains largely decentralized to give as much power as possible to the front lines of its various markets. Nestlé's country managers are extremely powerful people: They decide local brands and product mixes, they have a strong say in how local manufacturing plants are run, and they are usually the ultimate decision-makers when it comes time to make changes in corporate strategic direction. Certainly, this is not a position for the faint of heart. In fact, Nestlé's list for attributes of successful managers reads more like a description for a trauma surgeon than a regional business manager: "courage, solid nerves and composure; capacity to handle stress."[1]

In terms of culture, Nestlé has set organic growth as its yardstick for success: Each business unit and country is measured primarily on real, internal growth. Unlike many publicly traded companies, Nestlé looks at the performance of a business unit on a medium- to long-term time frame. In fact, when it reorganizes or carries out other equally sensitive strategies, Nestlé often sets implementation time lines in terms of five-year periods, which is unheard of in other companies. Such behavior underscores a key point: Nestlé is committed to the concept of gradual, continuous improvement and avoids dramatic one-time changes or sudden disruptions.

Nestlé is an example of a top-performing company that is stretching its growth along many dimensions simultaneously. Although there aren't many companies that are as good as Nestlé, there are many good companies stretching their growth prospects in interesting and innovative directions. The path for companies that have reached this point is clear and logical: They must look to their hidden assets—customers, brands, product know-how, channel position, knowledge management, external networks, and value chain—to make the final, strategic stretch.

To better illustrate this final step, we'll look at nine examples of stretch growth levers and show how best-practice companies are using them to push past traditional barriers and reach new heights. Not all of the examples are in the same league as Nestlé, but each company has achieved impressive growth results and offers a compelling story. Similarly, not all of the stretch growth levers may resonate with your company's current competitive situation, but we hope that at least some may help spark a new stretch growth idea.

VALUE CHAIN AND BUSINESS MODEL

Every so often, a company comes up with a new approach that completely transforms the way an industry is perceived. European furniture retailer IKEA became one such company when it effectively and profoundly redefined its industry's value chain. Traditionally, furniture retailers have a showroom where customers can browse; after the customer purchases a piece, the retailer calls the warehouse, which delivers the item to the customer's home a few days later (or four to eight months later in the case of custom and high-end furniture retailers). The delivery person is also responsible for any assembly that the piece requires. IKEA, on the other hand, combines the warehouse and the showroom into one. Customers select the exact piece of furniture they want and take it home with them. If assembly is required, they do it themselves. It's a win-win situation: Customers enjoy greater convenience, and IKEA enjoys tremendous cost savings.

In other scenarios, a company might identify a specific part of an industry's value chain and leverage and expand it until it becomes an industry of its own. That is what Mylan Laboratories, the premier U.S. generic pharmaceutical company, has done. Founded in 1961, Mylan realized that pharmaceutical companies were making a fortune from products even after their patent protection had expired. From this realization, Mylan became one of the first companies in the world to build its business around contract manufacturing. After a product's patent protection ends, Mylan manufactures the generic version and sells it for a fraction of the cost of the name brand. This has evolved into a significant industry in the United States and has proven valuable to health-care providers and consumers alike in reducing the cost of pharmaceutical products.

Finally, sometimes a company discovers that it has a hidden jewel in its value chain—one that can lead it into new business directions and growth. Consider Amazon.com, a company that most people still consider to be an online bookseller. But a few years ago, Amazon realized that the software that powers its online bookstore was extremely valuable. Consequently, it launched two supplementary lines of business. The first is the Merchants.com Program, in which Amazon supplies e-commerce services and features to power other companies' web sites, including Target, the large U.S. retailer. The second line of business is the Syndicated Stores Program, in which Amazon supplies e-commerce services and features to sell its products on other companies' web sites. Companies such as Borders, Virgin Mega, CDNOW, and Walden Books have all signed up for this. The result is that Amazon has increased its distribution channels while earning license and royalty fees at virtually no incremental cost.

CUSTOMER BASE

Leading companies often realize the wealth potential that can be found in their customer bases and, consequently, become eager to understand what customers really want. Should I be selling other products or services? Are my customers going elsewhere? How can I increase the value achieved from each customer?

German discount retailer Aldi is a good example of a company that stretched its customer base as a means to grow. Aldi is currently the leading discounter in Germany and is growing quickly in neighboring countries including Austria, Spain, the United Kingdom, and Denmark. Aldi began as a low-end, deep discounter, with a very explicit business model of selling high-quality products at the lowest price in the market. The tradeoff is no-frills levels of customer service and Spartan surroundings. Despite a somewhat turbulent ride in the 1970s, the company has continuously expanded both in terms of geography and product offerings.

Today, in light of Europe's recession, the company has expanded its customer base by appealing to higher income customers. It has created a new customer segment by becoming a hybrid retailer—serving its traditional low-end segment, while offering selected upscale products to capture a foothold among high income consumers. It offers, for example, top-quality champagne for just €9.95 per bottle, which helped increase its popularity among higher-income consumers, many of whom began serving ALDI champagne at parties.

But the main expansion of its customer base has been partly due to a unique advertising campaign that features deeply discounted items. For example, when a store announces a new campaign, such as a sale on computers or printers, the prices are so good that people begin lining up in front of the store before it opens to make sure they don't miss out on the sale.

Another example of stretching a customer base is currently taking place in the global banking and insurance industry. A number of banks and insurance companies are merging globally in an attempt to cross-sell their product offerings across the two industries. Citigroup's merger with Traveler's, Allianz's merger with Dresdner Bank, and Manulife's attempted takeover of the Canadian Imperial Bank of Commerce are all examples of this strategy in action. Unfortunately, at least in the Citigroup case, the premium paid for the acquisition doesn't yet appear to be justified by the results of the cross-selling of product lines.

The dental industry is also a burgeoning market for anyone interested in leveraging a customer base, particularly for those in the business of supplying products and services to dentists, dental laboratories, and dental institutions. The dental industry has always been known for its highly fragmented customer interface—most dental clinics have one or two dentists and a couple of hygienists. Yet, these little offices are served by many of the largest companies in the world, including General Electric, Siemens, and Johnson & Johnson. Filling the gap between these two uneven sides are companies such as Patterson Dental Supply, a leading dental distributor in North America. Patterson has built a large salesforce that works with dentists to access the best products and equipment to fit their business needs. Patterson also develops and sells office management software designed specifically for dentists and software to help dentists design the optimal office layout. The payoff for Patterson has been huge: It is one of the leading growth companies in the world, more than doubling sales revenue and profitability over the past five years alone.

SERVICE

Providing service at the right points in the customer experience cycle can win significant loyalty from customers and clear new paths to growth. Progressive Auto Insurance, for example, reengineered the customer service experience following a car crash. With most insurance companies, customers in an accident are left to their own devices to call the police and find a tow truck and medical services, if needed. Progressive, on the other hand, developed processes to take control of the crash site. When Progressive customers are involved in an accident, the company works with them to determine what assistance is needed. It dispatches emergency medical services, calls the police, and deploys a tow truck to the crash scene. Progressive also arranges for a rental car to be driven to the crash site for its customers and sorts out the numerous other details on behalf of their clients.

For the customer, Progressive takes much of the sting out of having an accident. For Progressive, it boasts among the highest levels of customer satisfaction and retention in the industry. And there are added side benefits to its innovative approach. By controlling which towing, repair, and rental-car services its customers use, Progressive consolidates its spend volumes and suppliers and significantly reduces its claims costs.

Schlumberger, the world's leading provider of oilfield services to large oil exploration companies, is another good example of how customer service and growth can go hand in hand. Schlumberger tests newly drilled oil exploration wells to determine how much oil they might produce in the future. This process requires a great deal of expertise, both by Schlumberger and by its clients, the multinational oil companies that interpret the data. One of the biggest challenges was how to transmit data from remote locations of the oilfields back to its clients. Schlumberger turned this inconvenience into a golden opportunity by developing extensive Web- and satellite-based communications and data-sharing capabilities that interpret and send test data from the oil well sites to the client for analysis. By providing these proprietary services, Schlumberger has effectively increased service levels to a point that none of its competitors can match.

PARTNERSHIP AND RISK SHARING

The best growth-oriented companies focus on their particular strengths and bring in business partners to fill in the gaps. Consider the partnership between Philips' small appliances and Sara Lee's Douwe Egberts coffee business. Their combined goal was to develop an innovative process to make the perfect cup of coffee. Noting that most families have large 8- or 12-cup coffee makers that are neither practical nor make a good cup of coffee, Philips and Sara Lee combined their expertise in coffee-making equipment and coffee ingredients to develop a new product called Senseo. Senseo makes "perfect" cups of coffee by brewing them fresh, one at a time, using coffee pads that come in different flavors. The Senseo machine has a relatively low price, and the individual coffee pads cost much less than a cup of coffee.

Senseo has been a runaway hit. Since its introduction in Holland in 2001, Senseo has captured a 10 percent market share. Philips and Sara Lee are now rolling it out across Europe. Another interesting dimension to this partnership is that both companies participate in the revenue stream generated by the sale of the coffee pads.

Too often, we see companies enter into partnerships that either go nowhere, or worse, end up in court. The approach taken by Philips and Sara Lee is innovative and new and can act as a benchmark for other companies that decide to use partnerships as a growth opportunity.

DISTRIBUTION CHANNELS

Stretch growth can also be realized through a solid distribution strategy. How many companies have lost their lofty positions by sticking too long with their legacy distribution channels? In the automotive and life insurance industries, for example, brokers have long been the bane of an insurance company's existence. The service quality from broker to broker is inconsistent, the broker distribution channel is expensive, and brokers hold all the vital information about an insurance company's customer base. In the mid-1990s, two insurance companies, Progressive and GEICO, emerged as industry leaders, both in terms of growth and profitability, largely because they distributed their insurance products directly to consumers and didn't bother with brokers. In doing so, they began to learn much more about the needs of their customers and could offer a much broader and tailored product range. It did not take long before their businesses expanded and both companies had taken market share away from their broker-based competitors and won industry-leading profits. When the established insurers tried to emulate Progressive's and GEICO's direct distribution channels, the already-rocky relationship between brokers and insurance companies was further exacerbated. In short, by thinking through the pros and cons of various distribution channels, Progressive and GEICO not only challenged the industry's status quo but emerged as its leading competitors.

Distribution strategy is tricky, though, and sometimes what appears to be a good plan on paper fails in practice. In the late 1990s, Ford Motor Company reconsidered its dealer-based distribution channel. The company began buying out its dealers in a number of markets as a way to create a direct sales channel. This strategy enraged and frightened its remaining dealers, who saw it as a direct threat from Ford and the precursor to Ford's competing directly against them. Adding fuel to the fire, Ford also began to experiment with a third potential distribution channel—selling cars directly over the Internet. When the strategy proved to be too bold for the industry and it failed, its champion within Ford, then-CEO Jacques Nasser, was fired. The lesson learned is that although a distribution strategy can be a powerful lever in creating growth, the decision to change models must be made and executed carefully.

BRANDS

Brands and branding strategy are another significant area for stretch growth. Every executive has heard the success story of Montblanc, the once-sleepy German brand for luxury fountain pens, ballpoint pens, and mechanical pencils. Montblanc products are easily recognizable by their white star logo, which represents the snow-peaked cap of the Mont Blanc mountain in France. Several years ago, Montblanc leveraged its already-strong brand name into cult status among luxury goods by establishing company stores in airports and shopping malls around the world.

It further enhanced its brand by establishing a line of collectible, limited-edition pens under names such as Catherine the Great, Mozart, and Edgar Allen Poe. Montblanc also expanded its product offerings to include leather items for business people, watches, and jewelry. Today, its products have become coveted status symbols. Indeed, for some executives, Montblanc pens and accessories are a sign that they have made it in their professional careers.

Now consider the stretch brand strategy of the Louis Vuitton-Moet Hennessey (LVMH) Group, which bills itself as "the world leader in luxury brands." LVMH's theory is that consumers associate a special status to any product in the LVMH family, whether the product is wine and spirits, fashion and leather goods, perfumes and cosmetics, or watches and jewelry. Consumers will pay a premium by virtue of the fact that the product is part of the

LVMH family. Consequently, LVMH carefully manages its portfolio of products and its distribution channels to ensure that this image is protected and upheld. It also owns high-end retailers DFS, Miami Cruiseline, Sephora, Le Bon Marché, and la Samaritaine that help maintain and reinforce its high-end positioning. LVMH's strategy for future growth is perhaps one of the most straightforward in the industry: Find high-quality products and brands that fit the LVMH style, and pump them through LVMH's marketing model and distribution channels.

CONVENIENCE AND CUSTOMIZATION

Breakthroughs in convenience and customization can also propel growth. Think about the brokerage industry before and after the advent of the Internet. Retail investing was traditionally based on a personal, consultative process between an investor and a stockbroker. Access to information about a particular investment was often limited to a company's annual report and whatever information a broker could provide. Then came the Internet. Today, online brokers such as E*Trade and TD Waterhouse make investing convenient, fast, and infinitely less expensive. Search engines such as Google and Yahoo! give retail investors immediate access to a plethora of investing information that was previously out of reach. Online investment information services and chat rooms such as the Motley Fool and The Street.com provide forums for investors to discuss investment ideas and interact with other investors. The entire process of retail investing has been transformed, mostly along the dimensions of convenience and customization. And, as with any change, the possibilities for new industries and innovative growth strategies abound.

The grocery industry is undergoing a similar, if somewhat less radical, transformation. Rather than driving to a grocery store, pushing a cart around endlessly searching for items that may or may not be in stock, and finally lugging the heavy grocery bags up your driveway and into your kitchen, online grocers such as Peapod in the United States and Grocery Gateway in Canada are transforming the industry. Grocery Gateway, for example, was formed in 1996 through venture capital funding and in partnership with a high-end Canadian produce and meat retailer. Customers place their orders online, specify a delivery time, and the groceries are delivered right to their kitchen counters. Because the markup and delivery charges are small, customers are switching in droves. The inconvenience and hassle of grocery shopping is gone.

GEOGRAPHIC REACH

Throughout the 1990s, geographic expansion became one of the most popular growth strategies. Asia, in particular, was a favorite destination for companies seeking to grow. After a certain point, however, the risk of expanding into the Asian market became relatively low, but so were the rewards. In fact, companies often found the same intense levels of competition in their new markets as they found back home. The best time to pull the geographic reach stretch lever is when a company can claim first-mover advantage.

An excellent example is AFLAC, the U.S. life insurance company. In 1974, the company, then known as the American Family Life Assurance Company of Columbus, was a small regional group life insurance company based in Georgia. But it had no intention of staying small. In fact, it became only the second foreign insurance company in history to be granted a license to sell insurance in Japan. Although the expansion was risky, AFLAC management seized the opportunity and aggressively expanded the business to Japan. Today, AFLAC is the largest foreign insurer in Japan and the second largest overall. AFLAC insures one in four Japanese households and, coincidentally, is the most profitable foreign company in any industry in Japan today. By getting in at an early stage, AFLAC was able to translate its core competencies from its home country business into competitive advantage in a new geographic market.

Another good example of first-mover advantage is Hewlett-Packard's expansion into China. HP opened its first representative office in China in 1981, allowing HP products and services to be sold there. This was the first partnership of its kind to be sponsored by the government of the People's Republic of China in conjunction with a foreign company. At the time, China was viewed as an unknown, risky place to invest, and HP's competitors did not immediately follow suit. But HP invested heavily in China, and today, despite the proliferation of Western goods and services across China, most Chinese government leaders and businesspeople remember HP's early commitment to their country.

TECHNOLOGY

The final stretch growth lever is technology. Technology's role in transforming business processes—and entire industries—can hardly be underestimated. The invention of the automobile wiped out the buggy whip industry, just as the invention of the refrigerator eliminated the need for an ice distribution industry. In recent times, the Internet has played a significant role in transforming existing industries and creating new ones.

Consider the time-honored business of auctions. At a consumer level, eBay has used the Internet to create an online auction juggernaut. Almost anything can be—and indeed has been—sold on eBay. In the process, the antiques business, used car business, used electronics and computers business, and a host of others have been completely revolutionized. In bringing online auctions to the masses, eBay has demystified and simplified the buying and selling process, prompting many consumers to spend considerable time—and money—on the site.

At the same time, eBay has created a huge amount of growth. Its revenues grew from US$86 million in 1998 to US$1.2 billion in 2002; its profits took a similar trajectory, going from US$7 million to US$249 million over the same period. Meanwhile, traditional auction competitors such as Sotheby's and Christie's have been left in the dust.

Another, more ambitious, use of technology to transform an industry and create stretch growth can be found in the business education industry, where a Singapore-based company, Universitas 21 Global, is building an Internet-based university that will provide business training and grant MBA degrees to students online. Universitas 21 is a consortium of Thomson Learning and 16 leading universities, including the University of Virginia (U.S.), McGill University (Canada), the University of Melbourne (Australia), the University of Birmingham (United Kingdom), the National University of Singapore, and the University of Hong Kong. Universitas 21 planned to begin online classes in the fall of 2003. Although it is too early to tell whether its business model will be successful, this exciting use of technology is a strong example of technology's potential to create stretch growth opportunities.

Now, let's tie these stretch growth concepts together with a case study of Johnson & Johnson. This powerhouse company has consistently led its industry in identifying its growth levers and developing and executing strategies around them. As a result, Johnson & Johnson has achieved superior business performance and financial returns for several decades.

JOHNSON & JOHNSON

Many of the attributes of Johnson & Johnson's growth track record are similar to Nestlé's. Started in the mid-1880s, Johnson & Johnson's founder, Robert Wood Johnson, developed the predecessor of Band-Aids by inventing a ready-to-use surgical dressing. Over the years, the company continued to grow and even expanded internationally with this single-product focus. In the 1920s, however, the founder's son, General Robert Wood Johnson, sought to change the company's future direction. In doing so, he developed Johnson & Johnson's credo—its guiding principles for how it would grow its business and what business practices it would embrace.

At the forefront of its growth strategy was a plan to diversify its products; decades later, this strategy remains at the core of the company's growth. At the time, it had to start small. It embarked on its diversification program by branding two consumer products, Band-Aids and Johnson's Baby Powder. This strategy led to decentralization and Johnson & Johnson's corporate philosophy that individual businesses must have the autonomy to pursue their own growth platforms. This freedom has been a mainstay throughout the company's history and has proved to be a powerful source of growth. In recent years, for example, the company has expanded aggressively into new growth areas such as biotechnology and specialty pharmaceutical product lines, and its hospital supply business has been transformed to focus on higher margin, higher growth medical equipment and diagnostics. Figure 10.2 illustrates Johnson & Johnson's flexible approach to business.

Like Nestlé, Johnson & Johnson built strong global franchises. It was one of the first U.S. companies to successfully acquire and integrate European businesses. In fact, in a number of instances—including its acquisition of Belgium-based Janssen Pharmaceutica—the acquired European business ultimately managed the

FIGURE 10.2   JOHNSON & JOHNSON'S GROWTH PORTFOLIO

Johnson & Johnson		
Product line	**Major brands/product lines**	**Notable acquisitions**
Consumer	Band-Aids Imodium Tylenol Contact lenses Janssen Baby powder Ortho-McNeil Birth control pills	Neutrogena
Pharmaceutical	Antifungal Neurology Anti-infective Oncology Cardiovascular Pain management Hematology Urology Immunology	ALZA Centocor Joint venture with Merck Scios Tibotec-Vicro
Medical devices and diagnostics	Wound care Artificial joints Surgical products Contact lenses Diagnostic Medical supply products business	Cordis DePuy Innovasive Devices Inverness Medical Technologies Obtech Medical

Source: www.jnj.com, A.T. Kearney analysis.

growth and market development for the business segment globally. Johnson & Johnson was also one of the first companies to invest heavily in China and Russia as their economies were opened to foreign investment.

However, the Johnson & Johnson approach to international business management is markedly different from Nestlé's. Johnson & Johnson generally develops its marketing and manufacturing strategies in the upper levels of the company, whereas Nestlé develops such strategies at its grass-roots levels.

As we mentioned earlier, at the center of Johnson & Johnson's business operations is the Johnson & Johnson credo. The credo, written by General Johnson more than 50 years ago, states the company's business objectives as being responsible to the interests of customers first, employees second, the community and the environment third, and shareholders fourth. General Johnson firmly believed that if the first three responsibilities are met, shareholder returns would always follow. Its credo has served Johnson & Johnson well, particularly during the Tylenol tampering crisis in the 1980s, when senior management quickly decided to clear the shelves of the product to protect consumers, even though they knew that the tampering was only an isolated incident. This adherence to the credo's spirit saved the Tylenol brand and reinforced Johnson & Johnson's image as a safety-conscious company in the minds of consumers.

Johnson & Johnson has also made use of mergers as a key growth strategy. Unlike Nestlé, which generally buys companies in mature, consolidating industries, Johnson & Johnson often buys companies in emerging, high-growth industries.

The most recent merger focus for the company was on biotechnology, where Johnson & Johnson paid billions for two leading companies, ALZA and Scios.

Despite the enormous size and diversity of Johnson & Johnson's history and its current business scope, the company's leadership has been remarkably stable. The company has had only seven chief executive officers in its history, and the founding family has been involved with the company since its inception. This continuity has undoubtedly contributed to the company's re-markable growth record. How remarkable? Its sales revenues have increased each year for 70 consecutive years, dividends have increased for more than 40 consecutive years, and the company has had 18 consecutive years of double-digit increases in earnings. The company is the global market share leader in medical devices and contact lenses and is the third-largest pharmaceutical company in the United States.

At the same time, its corporate reputation is immaculate. The company is one of the few large global companies to have a triple A credit rating, *Fortune* magazine ranks it as the sixth most admired company in America, and a 2003 Harris Interactive/*Wall Street Journal* poll ranks it as having the best corporate reputation in America for the fourth straight year.

Both Nestlé and Johnson & Johnson have overcome a number of hurdles of the stretch stage. They feature remarkably flexible business models, strategies, and operating philosophies that have allowed them to build dominant global franchises. Their business results have been powerful, and they show no signs of letting up.

This chapter concludes the profiles of the four growth steps. We now turn to the question of how to realize the benefits of these growth steps in your company. In the next part, we discuss how to develop strategies and implementation tactics, regardless of your company's industry position. We then discuss how to organize implementation teams and get ready for the changes that will occur as your company strives for a new, accelerated, and more profitable growth trajectory.

PART IV

EXECUTION AND CONCLUSION

CHAPTER 11

Organizing for Growth: Resourcing Implementation Considerations

No matter what industry your company is in, your financial position, or your competitive ranking, growth is often determined by the softer management issues:

- How growth oriented are your people?

- Is your senior management team aligned on the need for growth? On the plan to achieve it?

- Does your board of directors endorse your growth plan? Does it accept the risks involved?

- How do your shareholders view your growth plan? How tolerant will they be of setbacks?

These are all tough questions to answer, but they must be addressed before a successful growth strategy can be launched and executed. In this chapter, we focus on precisely these issues and offer advice on how to conceive, position, and execute the intangible aspects of a growth strategy. Before beginning, though, it is time to take stock of your company's starting position. The following quiz will help identify the point at which your growth journey should begin and where some of the roadblocks and pitfalls may lie:

1. My company has a well-defined growth strategy that takes into account our financial and competitive position, as well as the growth prospects and dynamics of our industry. ☐ Yes ☐ No

2. We have tested the key tenets and assumptions embedded in our growth strategy with our customers, suppliers, distribution channel partners, and other important constituencies, and they appear supportive and aligned. ☐ Yes ☐ No

3. My company's board of directors has spent a significant amount of time reviewing and understanding our growth strategy and strongly supports it. ☐ Yes ☐ No

4. My executive management team has been integrally involved in developing our growth strategy and strongly supports it. ☐ Yes ☐ No

5. Rank and file employees have been made aware of the new impetus for growth in our company and of the new actions and behavior expected as a result of growth strategy. ☐ Yes ☐ No

6. We have reviewed the capabilities and skills of our leadership team against the key needs and criteria required for the successful execution of our growth strategy, and we appear to have good coverage. ☐ Yes ☐ No

7. We have reviewed the growth strategy with our major shareholders (and equity analysts), and they appear to be supportive. ☐ Yes ☐ No

Although this checklist may seem fairly basic, in our experience, the majority of companies that embark on a major growth strategy typically answer yes to only two or three of these questions. We are not suggesting that companies must be able to answer yes to all of the questions before beginning, but we do recommend having an action plan in place to cover all of your bases. Otherwise, it may be difficult to attain all of the results possible.

With the starting point in mind, the rest of this chapter walks through strategies for gaining support and commitment from your major constituencies—the people who will carry out and implement your growth strategy.

GAINING THE CONVICTION FOR GROWTH

Resuscitating a company's drive for growth begins at the top, usually at the board of directors. The board's impact in executing a growth strategy is twofold: On one hand, individual board members may have valuable experience to share; on the other hand, the board must endorse the growth strategy on behalf of the company's shareholders.

Does your board of directors have the necessary skills and experience to be of value to your company's growth strategy? Often the answer is no, especially in small or privately held companies. Board members are frequently chosen based on personal relationships and may not have sufficient exposure to international markets or new product launches, for example, to offer valuable perspectives when it comes to making strategic decisions. In some instances, it may be necessary (and correct) to recruit new board members with the requisite skills.

Once you have a well-rounded, experienced board in place, members should spend time with management to gain a better understanding of the key aspects of the growth strategy. This allows board members to become comfortable with the plan, confident that it is well thought-out, and is in the best interests of shareholders. Bet-the-farm growth strategies and strategies predicated on major acquisitions, for example, should be subject to intense scrutiny by board members. Board members should be equally intent on ensuring that a strong organic growth engine is in place in all of the company's major business units.

The executive leadership team is another constituency that must be an integral part of the development and execution of a growth strategy. We often see companies that develop their growth strategies in a vacuum, created by either the CEO or members of the strategic planning department, who then hand the plan over to line managers to execute. This type of growth strategy does not work and often leads to disaster.

Rather than working in a vacuum, companies should adopt an all-inclusive approach. Senior executives should work closely with business-unit leaders to brutally and honestly hammer out a growth strategy. They should assess the current competitiveness of their businesses, brainstorm ideas and screen growth opportunities, and develop and execute action plans for the most promising opportunities. Proper execution of such a process should occupy the attention and commitment of the entire senior management team and be stress-tested through peer reviews.

Perhaps the best example of an all-inclusive approach is General Electric's annual budget reviews under CEO Jack Welch. Once a year, the leaders of each of General Electric's major lines of business would come together in an open forum to present their annual growth plans. Once a plan was presented, everyone had a chance to ask questions and offer critiques, including Jack Welch. These meetings were highly political and could make or break a career, but, at the end of the day, business-unit leaders had received valuable input and guidance from the best minds in the company and went home with solid, achievable growth objectives.

One interesting facet of these meetings was that each business in General Electric's portfolio was assigned a role, or designation, based on its contribution to General Electric's overall growth. *Harvest* businesses were in mature industries. Because they had limited growth prospects, these businesses were managed to generate maximum cash to pay for growth initiatives in others areas of the company. *Grow* businesses, as you might suspect, had good growth prospects and were expected to grow aggressively and steal market share from competitors. *Invest* businesses were the promising businesses of the future, so they were actively funded for the purpose of building dominant market positions for future growth. Leaders of each business unit were then measured on their ability to meet the objectives of their designated units—heads of grow business units, for example, were measured by their ability to meet specific growth targets.

Once the growth strategy has been developed and agreed to by the executive team, the strategy must be *embedded* into the modus operandi of the company (many executives refer to this as *walking the talk*). The importance of this step cannot be overstated. It is not unusual to come up with a great growth strategy, only to later find it collecting dust on the shelf of the (former) CEO.

Embedding a growth strategy requires several fundamental tasks, including:

- Assess the governance model to make sure that the growth strategy will be implemented over the long term. This can take shape with a simple reallocation of responsibilities for performance evaluations, for example, shifting responsibility for performance reviews from the CEO to the shared responsibility of the CEO and the compensation committee of the board.

- Review performance objectives and compensation processes to ensure they offer incentives for behavior linked with the growth strategy.

- Develop and implement a communication plan to rank-and-file employees so they understand the new growth strategy and the requisite actions and behaviors that go along with it.

- Develop action plans to gain the support, commitment, and partnership of suppliers, customers, and distribution channel partners to carry out the necessary tasks (from their perspective) to implement the growth strategy.

SELECTING THE RIGHT CEO FOR GROWTH

For companies committed to rejuvenating growth, the selection of the CEO is vital.

Following the boom years of the late 1990s, many boards of directors began to rethink their CEO selection strategies because growth had stalled for these companies. And it was little wonder given that a large number of CEOs had either been ineffective or one-trick wonders.

The one-trick-wonder syndrome has been particularly detrimental to growth. As economic conditions deteriorated, companies turned to cost-cutting strategies to meet their commitments to Wall Street. And a rash of well-known CEOs became known for their cost-cutting prowess. Unlike growth, which is difficult to achieve and measure, cost-cutting is tangible and the results are easy to obtain and to see. On the other end of the growth pendulum were CEOs whose penchants for large, value-destroying mergers became legendary. Regrettably, the majority of CEOs who espouse cost-cutting or big M&As never understand how to cultivate and embed growth engines into the companies they lead.

In the current low-growth economic climate, we are seeing a return to the truly strategic CEOs of yesteryear. Remember Lou Gerstner of IBM and Stanley Gault of Goodyear? Both were true leaders who redefined the value chains of their companies and pioneered new growth engines for the future prosperity of their shareholders. Gerstner recognized that new growth levers represented the future for IBM and completely reconfigured the company's business model to build its high-growth, high-margin software and professional services businesses while allowing the commodity-like hardware business to decline. Gault pushed Goodyear aggressively into international markets and transformed the basis on which Goodyear competed, moving it from a high-cost, high-differentiation business model to a low-cost, broad-distribution global leader.

That both Gerstner (ex-American Express) and Gault (ex-Rubbermaid) were recruited from the outside is not important.

We mention this only because there are some who think the best CEOs come from outside a company. When it comes to growth, however, we argue that unless completely necessary, the most appropriate CEO candidates to lead new waves of growth usually come from inside a company. To build and nurture the sort of growth engine found at Johnson & Johnson or Nestlé, for example, a CEO must have excellent knowledge of the strength of the strategic and organization levers available at his or her disposal. For outsiders, this is often difficult knowledge to acquire.

Equally important, the most successful growth companies build and refine their growth models gradually, extracting value over decades, not quarters or years. Outsiders generally have a shorter perception of the time frame over which they need to produce results, which is often not conducive to establishing an enduring growth-oriented business model. Insiders are generally more appreciative and respectful of the growth prospects and capabilities inherent in a company's business model.

Again, the board of directors must be heavily involved in the CEO selection process. Starting with the precepts that have made the company successful over its history, the board should create a list of criteria to screen and evaluate CEO candidates, and all board members should be actively involved in the selection process.

Finally, board members should draw up clear criteria for evaluating CEO performance. Although it is difficult to quantify an enduring growth model, it can (and should) be done. Long-term measures such as market share, 5- or 10-year-growth track records, and global competitive position will help to assess the strength of a company's growth model. These longer term measures will also help balance the often used short-term measures of EPS, EBITDA, and other annual, static measures.

Sometimes the evaluation requires tough decisions. This was the case for one board of directors whose CEO had been in place for more than 10 years and had led the company to record profits each year. But as the industry matured, the company needed a new business model—one that required innovation and some risk-taking. The CEO, who had been so successful using the old business model, was reluctant to change. Because he was slated for retirement in two years, he wanted to continue on a safe course that would continue to achieve record profits.

But board members, recognizing the need to immediately capitalize on the longer term growth imperatives, decided to bring in a deputy CEO. The CEO continued to focus on maximizing the profitability and performance of the core business, while the deputy positioned the company for future growth and was in line to succeed the CEO on his retirement.

ESTABLISHING A GROWTH CULTURE

Several intangible actions contribute to form a successful growth culture. Walk down the corridor of a company that has strong, sustainable growth, and you will notice several things:

- Employees generally have a greater sense of pride and belonging and can usually relate how a specific activity fits into the growth model of the overall company.
- Employees are more acutely aware of the company's market position, the strengths and weaknesses of its major competitors, and the prospects for growth in the marketplace.
- Employees are used to breaking through organizational silos to work across functions or business units to accomplish growth initiatives.
- Management walks the talk and espouses the growth values that the company is trying to accomplish in the marketplace.

On the surface, these concepts seem nebulous and difficult to accomplish. How is it possible to get rank-and-file employees to understand their company's competitive position? Jack Welch told General Electric employees that if their business was not first or second in global market share, they would be divested. You can be certain that every single General Electric employee knew exactly where the business stood in terms of competitiveness. The challenge is for senior management and the CEO to think through what messages need to be sent and reinforced to build a growth culture.

Walking the talk is a particularly important management principle that is critical for a successful growth strategy. But it is particularly difficult to define and to hold managers accountable for. Senior management teams must spend a great deal of time together to understand what walking the talk means and how to reinforce that type of behavior. When done well, it can achieve wonders within a company; when done poorly, or sporadically, it can be disastrous.

One excellent starting point for walking the talk is in the area of embedding organizational flexibility and prudent risk-taking. Once a growth strategy is put in place, companies usually develop a portfolio of growth initiatives. Some initiatives are almost certain to result in growth, but others have a higher standard deviation of potential outcomes. If management is to walk the talk, it should be prepared, for example, to punish a manager who delivers mediocre results on a high-probability growth initiative and reward a manager who executes flawlessly on a higher risk growth initiative that does not pan out.

Another test of a good growth strategy is how committed the management team is to sticking with the strategy even in rough times. In a recent survey conducted by A.T. Kearney, 53 percent of CEOs wrote in their annual letter to shareholders that top-line growth was one of the top three strategic initiatives for the company in the coming year. However, our experience has been that growth plans are often shelved or critical investments to achieve growth are often postponed if earnings projections hit a rough patch. This is why the board of directors must be actively involved in the development of a growth strategy. The board must be able to represent to management how patient investors will be for the growth strategy to produce results, how investors will react to risks in the growth strategy, and how much investors will be willing to spend on realizing future growth. If these parameters are well understood from the outset, management has a much better chance at succeeding with its growth strategy.

A final test for walking the talk is in the commitment of senior management to structured knowledge transfer. As we saw in the Johnson & Johnson case study, J&J's growth strategy is predicated on the systematic, seamless transfer of knowledge and best practices from one of its many lines of business to another. To take advantage of this growth tool, senior managers must be prepared to free up their best resources for training and participation in cross-functional teams, no matter how much the loss of these key resources may affect the business in the short term. They must be prepared to involve their customers in initiatives to develop new products or services no matter how painful the criticisms for past performance lapses might be. And they must be prepared to overcome the not-invented-here syndrome and accept that others' ideas may be better than their own.

The final piece to the growth-culture puzzle is managing shareholder expectations. In the current economic downturn, a number of leading blue chip companies have seen the maturation of their growth strategies, while watching their future long-term growth prospects and growth rates for their industries fall. Shareholders of Coca-Cola, McDonald's, Procter & Gamble, and others had become accustomed to 10 percent growth per year in the past. With these growth rates less certain for the future, meeting Wall Street expectations is becoming increasingly difficult. At the same time, the penalty for a drop in share price or for underperforming on an earnings commitment has increased. As a result, several companies are eliminating quarterly earnings forecasts or resorting to other means of diffusing the short-term variability of their growth prospects.

Shareholders must be educated. They should have a strong understanding of the competitiveness and growth strategy of the company they are investing in. The CEO and management team must explain to shareholders how they are managing and strengthening the growth levers, what risks they see to the growth levers in the future, and what new areas of growth they have identified and plan to pursue. In addition, management should put forward some long-term performance measures (as well as short-term measures) that shareholders can use to judge the company's long-term growth performance and track record.

ORGANIZING FOR GLOBALIZATION AND GEOGRAPHIC EXPANSION

Once a company finalizes its list of growth initiatives, organization structures are inevitably created, or redrawn, to properly deploy resources to the new opportunities. Among the most complex decisions is how to organize for geographic expansion or globalization of a business. In this section, we shed some light on strategies for organizing international growth.

The success of an international business organization depends on the following:

- Depth of the *bench strength* of international management experience.
- The reporting lines and organizational structure used to link the corporate organization with the field.
- Management approach for emerging markets versus mature markets.

Management's bench strength is often viewed as a showstopper for many companies contemplating international growth. Small- and medium-sized companies, in particular, are often intimidated by this challenge. As a result, they often make mistakes, either by ceding too much control of their business model (or margin) to a local distributor or business partner or by becoming overwhelmed by the daunting challenge of the entire exercise and not expanding at all.

High-performing companies plan far in advance for international expansion. They actively identify and groom managers who have an interest in running an international business or who have previous international business experience. In Asia, Citigroup has a multiyear management development program designed to identify and develop local business leaders through a structured series of rotational assignments in the country and in major global money centers. This program is legendary in Asian business circles and has resulted in Citigroup's having local (not expatriate) country presidents in each of the major Asian countries—something that none of its competitors can come close to matching.

Choosing the organizational structure for international businesses is either a major pitfall or a source of competitive advantage. Some companies turn over the responsibility of international expansion to global business-unit leaders. The problem with this approach is that managing a global business forces the leader to focus on only the biggest, most important markets. In the auto parts industry, for example, global business-unit leaders would expand into the major European markets and Japan. However, although important developing markets such as China, India, and South Korea might be critical to future growth in 5 or 10 years, they may not be big enough today to make a material impact on the performance of a giant global business unit.

Another pitfall—for companies that have a predominant or single product line—is the possibility of a strong bias toward corporate control of core competencies on a global basis. In the consumer products industry, for example, this would translate into corporate dictating key marketing and brand messages, with little regard for the needs and nuances of individual, country-specific considerations. Although this approach is often appropriate for the early stages of geographic expansion, it can stifle growth after a certain point.

A better way to develop an international organization is for the senior management team to think through its international organization structure, thinking in terms of where it wants to control the key elements of its value chain. Companies should consciously and actively choose whether a local, regional, or global organization is required for each important component of its value chain. For example, parts procurement for an aerospace or automotive company is probably best done at a corporate or global level organizationally to consolidate procurement volumes and reap maximum benefits of economies of scale. Also the selection and management of brand portfolios in the consumer products business is probably best done at the country or regional level because local managers will have the best understanding of consumers' tastes and preferences, price points, and competitive positioning.

Companies that are expanding rapidly in international markets sometimes face the challenge of overstretching their scarce resources, particularly when it comes to senior management. Some companies use a technique called *dual-hatting* to leverage their senior managers' capabilities during rapid growth periods. Dual-hatting leverages the international experience of senior line managers by making them accountable for both country-specific and regional business objectives. Imagine, for example, a pharmaceutical company where a line manager is responsible for both the financial performance of the Japan business, as well as the marketing for a certain product line across Asia. Other managers would be deployed in similar fashion across the region. The organizational leverage occurs by having most senior managers focus both on individual country performance and region-wide performance for a specific set of products. Done well, this can create a healthy tension across the region in which management negotiates trade-offs to achieve its product and market-growth objectives across a region. For example, one manager might trade a price concession on Product A in one country for a print advertising campaign on Product B in another country.

In general, though, dual-hatting is used only during transitions, and it can help to leverage scarce management talent during rapid growth periods while allowing the company to develop local management talent and succession plans.

The final international growth challenge from an organizational standpoint is how to manage growth in emerging markets compared to mature markets. Anyone with experience in international business will talk at length about the challenges of emerging market growth: low affordability levels and inability to price to international levels, intense local competition, and foreign equity ownership restrictions, to name a few. An insightful exercise is to plot the penetration rate of your company's product or service in a given country versus the GDP per person of that country. For added effect, add a bubble for each country, whose size is proportional to its population. The case for emerging market growth will be immediately apparent—the largest countries in the world will likely have the lowest penetration rates for your product.

However, deciding which emerging markets to place bets on and a realistic time frame for results is more difficult. One thing is certain—it will almost always take longer than you expect to achieve the hoped-for results. Consider, for example, that almost every multinational has invested heavily in China over the past decade, yet very few have ever made a profit there. Companies believe they must be in China because of China's large population, falling trade barriers, and growing affluence. Yet, finding a profitable business model for China is proving to be elusive. Therefore, in a growth strategy for an emerging market, have more patience and tolerance for delays.

There are almost an infinite number of people and organizational considerations that must be addressed to realize the benefits of a successful growth strategy. We have tried to capture the major topics here but also stress that a well-thought-out, thorough, integrated approach to organizing for growth is worth much more than the sum of the parts.

Equally important to a successful growth strategy are the business processes that support and enable it. In the next chapter, we look more closely at some of the most critical business processes that can make or break a growth strategy. We offer advice and examples of how best practice companies structure important business processes to boost their growth prospects.

CHAPTER 12

Reengineering Your Business Processes for Growth

The goal of any growth strategy is to build capabilities, competencies, and processes within your company that can produce growth in a manner that is defensible against competition and will be sustainable over time. This is the *growth engine* that we referred to earlier.

In this chapter, we offer more details about the key steps required to build a growth engine. We begin with a short checklist to gain a better understanding of your company's starting position. The following should help identify the current state of your Value-Building Growth processes, including areas of strength that can be leveraged and areas that need to be bolstered for your company to grow in the future:

1. We continually assess the effectiveness of our basic growth processes to ensure that they are achieving the objectives of our growth strategy.   ☐ Yes   ☐ No

2. My company has an innovation process that includes all the right people.   ☐ Yes   ☐ No

3. My company reviews its portfolio of growth opportunities formally once a year and provides our board of directors with progress updates.   ☐ Yes   ☐ No

4. We constantly search for attractive acquisition candidates, and we have a formal review process to ensure that any contemplated acquisition helps us to achieve our growth strategy.   ☐ Yes   ☐ No

5. We have a well-established team and set of processes to integrate acquired companies.   ☐ Yes   ☐ No

As in the previous chapter, the statements on this checklist may appear obvious or simplistic. However, most companies can say yes to only one or two of the statements, whereas *stretch* growth companies can say yes to all five. This chapter suggests ways to move your company toward growth in each area. Specifically, we discuss how to prepare for growth by reengineering each growth lever, how to develop processes and methods for identifying new growth opportunities, how to chart a course (and time frame) to produce growth, and how to identify those opportunities that represent the best starting point for growth.

BASIC ENABLING PROCESSES

Through growth business process reengineering (BPR), we look at the basic processes in your company that contribute to (or detract from) achieving growth in your core business. These processes represent the bare bones, minimum requirements for growth in a competitive market. The key challenge is to accurately and honestly assess how well your company is performing against each. If there is a performance gap, you must implement a remedial action plan to close the gap. If your company is particularly strong in one or more areas, you should seek ways to bolster and leverage that strength competitively. Consider the following examples:

- Dell boasts superior performance in the areas of competitive pricing and timely availability, on which it has built its competitive advantage over the past 10 to 15 years. Southwest Airlines, the most profitable airline today, has used the same strategy in the airline industry.

- Nucor, the American steel company, built its business model around using recycled steel. In doing so, it reduced its cost position and transformed the global steel industry.

- Coca-Cola, McDonald's, and Nike leveraged their brand recognition to build formidable global growth franchises.

- Toyota's superior customer satisfaction levels made the Camry the top-selling car in the United States today.

How should you go about assessing your current position? Typically, a company starts by benchmarking, or measuring key performance indexes to find out where the company stands along several dimensions. Often, these benchmarks are measured against major competitors as well. A company looks at best practice processes used by companies in other industries to gain a perspective on what constitutes breakthrough performance. Either way, success depends on how the benchmark data is used. Remember, some benchmarks, especially qualitative, provide only directional information, not absolute information. The process of collecting benchmark data is rarely scientific (or statistically valid), and the interpretation can be highly subjective. Nonetheless, benchmarks can provide a good assessment of how competitive your company is on each of the major growth enablers and can serve as the starting point for a remedial strategy.

The second step in improving your company's basic growth enablers is to think strategically about how your industry will evolve in the next few years. Consider how your customers' needs will evolve. Are there any new technological developments, for example, that would (or should) cause your company to reevaluate its strategy? This is exactly what Microsoft has done in light of the Internet and the reason that Microsoft is now developing growth opportunities in web-based applications by means of its *dot-Net* growth strategy.

The third step to increasing growth from your core business is to focus on implementation and results. Companies with strong growth engines rarely resort to reactionary or step-change growth turnaround strategies. Instead, they foster a culture of continuous improvement in which employees are encouraged to focus on capturing growth opportunities on an ongoing basis. Companies must also take a holistic view of their entire value chain—from customers and suppliers to distribution partners—and include all parties in their efforts toward growth.

INNOVATION: THE BIRTH OF NEW PRODUCTS AND SERVICES

The most common source of incremental growth lies in the development of new products or services. Companies launch new products all the time, ranging from simple *line extensions* (minor enhancements to well-established existing products) to complete new offerings that can redefine an entire industry. Although there is no magic formula for coming up with the next great new product idea, there are a number of basic processes that will cultivate the development of new products and services.

The first process is often referred to as *anthropological observation*. Research shows that most new product ideas, or enhancements to old products, are the result of watching consumers use the product or service in their day-to-day lives. The ideal test ground is any place where you can observe consumers in a listening-intensive and familiar environment. A simple, but practical, example comes from a product design team at Pyrex. By observing professional chefs cooking with Pyrex measuring cups, the product design experts noticed that the chefs had difficulty picking up the cups because the handles were too small. By enlarging the handle and making it easier to grasp, Pyrex increased sales and boosted customer satisfaction.

A more complex example comes from Loblaw's, the Canadian grocery retailer highlighted in Chapter 6. Loblaw's wanted to provide its customers with a suite of financial services products—services that people would be likely to use while at the supermarket. Before proceeding with the idea, the supermarket chain conducted a series of complex consumer behavior and focus group research studies. Executives wanted to determine the range of financial services product offerings consumers would be most likely to use during a shopping trip. The findings pointed to a suite of offerings, including deposit and withdrawal services, personal lines of credit, and mortgages, which are now being offered under Loblaw's well-known President's Choice banner.

The second way to foster new ideas for products and services is to take an outside-in view of the steps and interrelationships involved in delivering a product or service to a customer. The idea is to gain a better understanding of all the possible influences on customer service. Our discussion of Progressive Insurance in Chapter 10 illustrated how the outside-in view can effectively drive new ideas. Progressive watched the sequence of events following an automobile accident. Rather than put its customers through the nightmarish situation that almost always follows an accident, Progressive established an accident-response center. Now, following an accident, drivers make a single call to the response center, which dispatches emergency medical services, deploys a tow truck to haul away the damaged vehicle, and even sends a rental car for the customer to drive away from the accident site.

This outside-in view is well suited to cross-functional brainstorming sessions. One approach is to include a series of brainstorming sessions in the regular agendas of your senior management team meetings. Once every two months or so, take a couple of hours to consider a particular growth theme or to take an outside-in view of a customer experience. If your company is focused on a single product, consider structuring the approach around different aspects of the product:

- How can the differentiating piece of technology in the product be leveraged? For example, if the package of a consumer product is truly state-of-the-art, how can it be leveraged to increase growth? Could a contract manufacturing subsidiary add growth?

- Are there peripheral products or services that can be added to the main offering? For example, if your company manufactures auto parts, can you add additional parts to connect the main part to the vehicle, for example? Can you offer a service of attaching the component to the body of the car in advance of production, rather than requiring the assembler to do it?

- Are there other industries that can use the core technology of your product or service? Remember how Teleflex (highlighted in Chapter 9) leveraged its aerospace cable technology by expanding into the medical equipment and automotive industries?

- Consider offering peripheral services around the broader need your product or service provides. For example, if you manufacture door locks, is there an opportunity to expand into door security systems to monitor who enters and exits through the door?

- It is easy to see how this broad approach can lead to several potential new directions for a single-product business, including the spawning of new start-up businesses or major acquisitions. Johnson & Johnson used a similar approach to identify opportunities to diversify into biotechnology and medical products—both are faster growing market segments that are used to supplement its core pharmaceutical and hospital supply businesses.

The third process for identifying new growth opportunities is to develop the value proposition for your product or service. *Value proposition* refers to how your product or service creates value for your customers. Frequently, companies segment their customer base and identify the value proposition for each segment. This not only fosters new ideas for expanding the range of products or services to a given segment, but also can lead to innovative pricing, which will allow you to capture more value from your customer segments.

Regardless of the method or methods that you use, there are many creative approaches for identifying new directions for growth in your company. If you are just starting out, try several processes until you find one that works.

GROWTH PORTFOLIOS

Once your senior management team has brainstormed and is armed with research on consumer tastes and usage patterns, you should be able to put together a list of potential growth opportunities. The sum of these growth opportunities is your *growth portfolio*—a collection of growth ideas and projects, all consistent with the overall growth strategy, which must be prioritized and then properly executed.

Prioritizing your growth opportunities is critical, requiring significant input and involvement from the senior management team. Typically, growth initiatives are prioritized against a rigorous set of criteria that usually revolve around time and complexity of implementation and financial cost and returns.

One leading company does an initial screening of its highest potential growth opportunities by qualitatively ranking the opportunity against the following criteria:

- Elapsed time to implement.
- People resources required to complete implementation.
- Investment capital required to complete implementation.
- Complexity and risk.
- Magnitude of anticipated financial return.
- Elapsed time until financial return is realized.

The management team uses this subjective criteria to prioritize the projects according to those with the highest growth potential and then turns the list over to implementation teams. Implementation teams spend the next few weeks defining implementation plans, assessing risks, and quantifying benefits. In light of the more detailed information, senior managers then recalibrate the prioritization list, deciding whether to proceed with each project. This process, which has been in place at the company for the past decade, is conducted twice a year.

MANAGING MERGER AND ACQUISITION DECISIONS

Once your company has built and nurtured a strong organic growth engine, it can be assured of its long-term growth prospects and will likely be rewarded by the stock market with a rise in share price. At this point, you should be the proud owner of what is often called *acquisition currency*. This occurs when share price is sufficiently high and the balance sheet is sufficiently strong to be used as "currency" for acquisitions.

Be careful, though. Just because you have the ability to make an acquisition doesn't mean you should. Typically, companies that make smart acquisition decisions do so in a discrete number of situations:

- From a make-versus-buy standpoint, the acquisition candidate allows you to accomplish your strategic and growth objectives faster and cheaper.
- Your industry is in a phase of rapid consolidation, and a bold stroke acquisition is the only way to either achieve or retain industry dominance.
- The acquisition price is a bargain.

Well-known serial acquirers such as Johnson & Johnson, GE Capital, Pfizer, and Nestlé, among others, have all used these strategies to their advantage. In most cases, the situations lead to a larger company acquiring a smaller company, which also leads to an easier postmerger integration process.

Most companies that have an active acquisition strategy build up strong internal M&A capabilities to address the weakest points in the M&A process. A recent A.T. Kearney survey of 360 CEOs of Fortune 500 companies concludes that executives place particular emphasis on developing a strategy (selecting the right acquisition candidates, for example) and ensuring a swift and thorough integration process.

In developing an M&A strategy, every company, regardless of its size, should put together a dream list of acquisition targets. Fortunes rise and fall, and no matter how much of a stretch an acquisition target may be for your company, at some point you may be able to make a move. We also advise our clients to be extremely thorough in the due diligence process. In addition to poring over the accounting and valuation reports, it is critical to conduct strategic and operational due diligence on each target acquisition. The success or failure of the acquisition may hinge on answering a few critical questions:

- What is the long-term sustainable growth rate of the target industry and the target company?

- How strong are the target's brands? How effective is its salesforce? How well is it perceived by customers, distributors, and competitors?

- How good is the target operationally? What is its quality record? What is its delivery record? Are its operations considered state-of-the-art or mediocre?

- How strong is the target's management team? How long has the team been in place? What is its reputation?

As a general observation, the most shareholder value is created when a larger, more successful company acquires a smaller, weaker player outright. This can be attributed to several factors, not the least of which is that smaller acquisitions are usually not bet-the-farm strategies; they are cheaper to finance and easier to integrate. Smaller, weaker players tend to fall into one of three generic strategies, depending on where the acquisition candidate is positioned on its industry value-building growth chart:

1. The lower left-hand corner represents a turnaround candidate, where swift, thorough integration is essential to reposition the acquisition into a more profitable, growing business model. GE Capital, for example, has made its reputation on acquisitions of this type.

2. The upper left-hand corner represents a margin enhancement candidate. Here the revenue growth model of the target is working well, but its cost structure does not permit it to be profitable. The M&A rationale is to increase the economies of scale, lower the acquisition candidate's effective cost structure, and, in so doing, increase overall margins.

3. The bottom right-hand corner is generally the most difficult acquisition because the integration imperative is to boost revenue growth. Success in making an acquisition of this type revolves around the successful implementation of the organic growth processes described earlier in this chapter. Most of the recent M&A activity in the pharmaceutical industry has been of this sort, with Pfizer's acquisitions of Pharmacia and Warner Lambert being prime examples.

Less successful M&A strategies tend to be carried out by acquirers that are not in the top right-hand corner of the Value-Building Growth Matrix. The prospects for this sort of M&A activity are not good. We often see *mergers of equals* (in other words, mergers of two underperforming companies) in which political turf battles and organizational infighting often bog down the integration process, usually at the expense of shareholder value creation. The mergers between AOL and Time Warner and between DaimlerBenz and Chrysler are prototypical examples.

Regardless of its rationale, once the acquisition has been completed, the integration process is the paramount driver of shareholder value. The bottom line is that all companies must develop a competency in integrating acquisitions in today's business environment. We anticipate a significant amount of industry consolidation to take place over the next decade, and the winners and losers in several industries may be determined by their internal capabilities at integrating acquisitions effectively. For a summary of the postmerger integration process, see the Seven Steps to Merger Success box.

The most impressive stretch growth strategy doesn't lead to results in the marketplace unless it is implemented effectively. In this part, we laid out techniques and strategies for turning stretch growth ideas and processes from *other* companies into growth action plans for *your* company.

We have presented tools and techniques for assessing the starting point for developing a growth strategy for your company that encompasses your current competitive and financial position. We provided advice and ideas on how to rejuvenate your leadership team and board of directors and focus them on growth. Finally, we recommended *stretch growth BPR* solutions for conceiving a growth portfolio of new growth ideas, both organic and acquisition-driven, for your company to pursue.

In the final chapter of the book, we offer our perspectives and predictions for the future prospects for growth in the months and years ahead.

SEVEN STEPS TO MERGER SUCCESS

The numbers are startling: More than half of mergers and acquisitions ultimately fail to create the value top management had envisioned. But heeding the pitfalls of the past is a big step toward a successful future. Analysis based on an A.T. Kearney survey completed in 1999 reveals that seven steps are key to making mergers work. Highlights of the research first appeared in the book, *After the Merger: Seven Rules for Successful Post-Merger Integration*, by Max

(continued)

Habeck, Fritz Kroeger, and Michael Träm (Financial Times/Prentice Hall, 2000).

1. *Create a clear vision and strategy.* Although companies devote a great deal of thought to strategy and vision when embarking on a merger, nearly 80 percent of companies place corporate fit ahead of corporate vision. Learning about a potential partner may win the battle; still, the companies that learn to live with one another are the ones that ultimately win the war.

Vision is the only acid test to determine whether companies are on the right track as they prioritize, execute, and interpret postmerger integration tasks. Many merging companies learn the hard way that fit flows from vision—not vice versa.

2. *Establish leadership quickly.* It is impossible to overestimate the importance of establishing strong leadership immediately when a merger deal is completed. The faster the merged company solidifies management—by working out compromises, minimizing or preventing defections, and making the most of available talent and knowledge—the faster it can exploit the growth opportunities inherent in its *one-business* vision. Yet, nearly 40 percent of all companies in the A.T. Kearney study faced a leadership vacuum because they failed to put the establishment of leadership at the top of the priority list. With no one to secure buy-in or provide a clear direction, conflicts simmer, decisions go unmade, and constituencies—from employees to customers to market analysts—lose patience.

3. *Merge to grow.* As important as cost-cutting and similar synergies are in mergers and acquisitions, they should be a secondary issue in the postmerger integration. It is clear that almost all mergers offer opportunities to save money. But the primary reason for the merger decision—and the obvious focal point during postmerger integration—should be growth. Merging companies must unlock the *merger added value* by taking advantage of the positive combinations offered by their combined resources. For example, the *growth* synergies identified during due diligence cannot be trumped

by *cost* or *efficiency* synergies. Companies run the risk of cutting too much and for too long.

In short, there are two kinds of synergies: *efficiency* and *growth*. Our survey shows where the emphasis currently—and unfortunately—lies. Some 76 percent of companies surveyed focused too heavily on the efficiency synergies. Some 30 percent of the companies surveyed virtually ignored attractive growth opportunities such as cross-selling possibilities or knowledge sharing in research and development.

4. *Focus on results and communicate them.* Merger announcements consistently spread uncertainty, not only among employees, but also among suppliers, customers, and shareholders. It is critical to inform stakeholders of plans and goals, but addressing these longer term issues is not enough. Companies need to also communicate early wins—successful and sustainable moves made quickly after the merger. This offers the audience the first glimmers of the potential of the deal. The result is solidified support and increased buy-in, both inside and outside the new company.

Where do early wins come from? Areas to consider inside the company include asset sales, knowledge sharing, and improvements   to the work environment. And there is a rich source of early wins in a place few companies look: outside the company. Relationships with suppliers or customers may improve after a merger—offering additional potential for positive communication.

Companies that look internally often fall into the trap of citing job cuts as early wins. Some 61 percent of merged companies search for early tread on dangerous territory by turning to job shedding, factory closings, or inward-looking cost moves. The negative emotions these moves produce can quickly turn them into *early losses.*

Fortunately, when business due diligence has been conducted properly, several sources of early wins should be readily apparent.

(continued)

5. *Be sensitive to culture clashes.* Cultural differences represent one of the most intractable problem areas in mergers and acquisitions, both before and after the deal is done. The term *culture* refers to a collection of elements, including behaviors, objectives, self-interest, and ego, that people are reluctant to discuss openly.

Successfully integrating cultures is key to making any merger work. When this challenge is approached in a structured way, it becomes more manageable.

When we looked at 115 transactions around the globe, we discovered one reason why many mergers are unsuccessful and why *cultural differences* are blamed. Cultural imposition is standard practice—whether it is the most appropriate strategy or not. Although this tactic is valid in some cases, in others it destroys the value the merger was supposed to create.

Problems frequently arise when the organizations that are coming together serve very different markets; in such cases, it is often best to leave the two cultures intact. If full integration of the two organizations is critical to release value, a *compound* culture should be created, one that takes the best elements from each of the parent organizations.

6. *Communicate throughout the process.* Managers who can persuade constituencies to believe in a vision and to act, fare much better at achieving their merger integration goals. In other words, the most compelling communicators come out ahead. This may appear to be the easiest aspect of merger integration. It's not. Communication doesn't just happen; managers must take responsibility, plan it carefully, and then control it over time.

Behind every effective communications program is a combination of communications goals, flexibility, and feedback. The effort is part art, part science—and often inadequate, as most companies acknowledge. Some 86 percent of respondents said that they failed to communicate their new alliance sufficiently in their merger integration phase.

For most companies, the biggest barrier to merger integration is failure to achieve employee commitment. Some 37 percent of respondents listed this as their primary challenge, well ahead of obstructive behavior and cultural barriers.

Successful companies emphasize their ultimate communications goal—a company that works seamlessly to realize the value of the merger. Taking this perspective encourages the deep-seated commitment required to achieve buy-in, provide proper direction and orientation, and properly manage expectations.

7. *Manage risks aggressively.* The most common reaction to risk is to avoid it. That's understandable. Risk carries a negative connotation in many people's minds. Unfortunately, any endeavor involving high returns and strong growth—including a merger—comes with comparably strong risks as well. Companies need to recognize and confront these risks instead of ducking them; when they do, they ultimately maximize the returns on the merger. Fortunately, the corporate world is acknowledging this need. Our global survey of 115 transactions showed encouraging signs that companies are making efforts to proactively face their risks. Some 32 percent of companies that are merging actively pursue formal risk management.

Effective risk management can lead to early wins. Some of these companies have developed enough expertise in risk management that it has become a source for both early wins and long-term growth.

Yet, on the other side of the coin are the two-thirds of all companies that integrate after a merger without the benefit of the risk management process. This statistic is alarming today—and will be more so tomorrow. In the future, the complexity of risk will grow in proportion to the opportunities large deals offer.

CHAPTER 13

Future Challenges for Growth

Throughout this book, we've recounted some of the greatest growth stories we know. We've also presented a straightforward four-step growth model that can help any company, any time, anywhere achieve growth. Looking back over the pages, it's possible that growth might seem easy. But, remember, if some of the world's best companies haven't been able to grow in recent years, it's for good reason. And, looking ahead, the growth challenge is not going to get easier.

Most of the world's largest economies are struggling with slow growth. In the United States and Europe, high levels of consumer and corporate debt and the hangover from burst asset bubbles and cratered stock markets mean the economy's natural growth momentum is not likely to change in the near future. In the United States, economists are predicting slow- to medium-growth rates until at least 2005. The predictions for Europe are for slower growth than the United States. In Japan, no one expects the national economy to improve dramatically without a bold, innovative government-sponsored change agenda. In the rest of Asia, however, especially in China, growth prospects seem promising. So, at best, the world economic climate for growth is lukewarm.

Meanwhile, the world continues to grapple with heightened risks from a variety of sources. The dangers of terrorism have existed for decades, but on September 11, 2001, they took on new meaning. The ripple effects from that day—and from the terrorist acts committed since then—continue to be felt around the world. The war in Iraq and ongoing tensions in the Middle East have increased friction between some countries in Europe and the United States. In line with this, the role of previously strong alliances such as the United Nations may diminish, if not disintegrate. The threat of the spread of diseases, such as SARS, mad cow disease (BSE), and the West Nile virus, dominate the news and, in turn, reduce corporate confidence in high-risk regions. Finally, economic dangers are also on the rise. Volatility in currency markets—such as the sharp decline of the U.S. dollar in early 2003—continues to wreak havoc for business planners and leisure travelers. The threat of deflation in several G-8 economies is significant, while unsustainable property prices in many countries ominously suggest the bursting of real estate market bubbles.

From a global trade perspective, the risk of increased levels of protectionism is high. The choppy geopolitical relationships among individual countries and regions raise the possibility that new rounds of World Trade Organization negotiations may collapse. The United States seems increasingly willing to use its size and power to favor its friends and allies and, in turn, make increased use of bilateral (rather than multilateral or global) trade agreements. At the same time, it seems less hesitant to resort to tariffs and trade restrictions when U.S. industries are threatened by foreign competitors.

Finally, a rapidly aging population in Japan and across many parts of Europe poses new challenges. Will Europe open its borders to immigration or face a significant aging of its population? How should companies plan for major demographic shifts and aging populations when research has established that older people prefer not to acquire physical goods, but instead buy services and experiences, such as travel and entertainment?

Beyond these geopolitical and macroeconomic factors, a number of management trends are at play that will also affect how companies create growth:

- Shareholder activism, class-action lawsuits, and new government regulations have raised the stakes for CEOs, boards of directors, investment banks, equity analysts, and other professional services providers.

- With the increased threat of lawsuits or even jail terms, the pool of potential business leaders and board members is shallow, and the incentives to lure the best and the brightest appear to be dwindling. The top candidates for corporate leadership positions and directorships simply don't want the jobs.

- In the United States, the recently enacted Sarbanes-Oxley Act presents new challenges and constraints on CEOs and boards of directors, particularly in time constraints and potential liabilities. At a recent conference hosted by A.T. Kearney, CEOs estimated that Sarbanes-Oxley would add 300 hours of extra work per year to their jobs—time they simply don't have, particularly when they need to focus on growth.

So, if there's any inclination to think that growth is easy, there is little that could be further from the truth. And we believe the current challenges merely hint at what is to come.

REASONS FOR HOPE

Despite these bleak forecasts, there is room for optimism. A strategic renaissance is taking place in companies around the world. Boards of directors are actively pursuing growth strategies and are once again devoting time and attention to core business fundamentals. CEOs are realizing that growth has little to do with magic formulas, brazen moves, and gut intuition and everything to do with strong operations, consistent strategies, and flawless execution.

We also predict renewed focus on growth in companies around the world. Management teams that have exclusively pursued cost-cutting strategies through the current economic downturn have likely cut costs to the bare bones and have brought growth to a standstill. They are now almost forced to use growth as the only remaining lever to move their companies forward. And, as we have seen throughout this book, examples abound of companies that have successfully met the growth challenge.

GROWTH PROSPECTS FOR MAJOR REGIONS

In the spirit of making predictions, we turn our attention to the future prospects of each major geographic region. Throughout the 1990s, North America—the United States in particular—led the way in growth, and it will likely continue to do so (see Figure 13.1). Despite a weak economy, the U.S. GDP continues to grow, albeit at a more modest rate. The stock market also appears to have stabilized and is showing signs of improvement based on recent corporate

FIGURE 13.1 REGIONAL POSITIONS ON THE VALUE-BUILDING GROWTH MATRIX

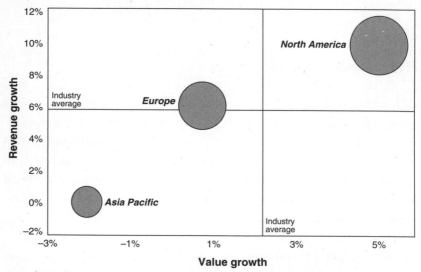

Note: Growth portfolio (CAGR 1997–2001) benchmarked against industry average.
Source: A.T. Kearney.

earnings reports. The falling U.S. dollar may boost U.S. exports and help improve profitability among U.S. multinationals. The prospect for deflation, particularly in property markets, is a possibility but does not appear to be as likely as in parts of Europe. Overall, the outlook for the United States seems reasonably good.

Europe's immediate future, on the other hand, seems more challenging. Stagnating economies in France and Germany, unemployment, protectionism, aging populations, significant overcapacity, the high euro, and the specter of deflation in many countries all bode poorly. Consider the euro. Its recent increase puts downward pressure on interest rates, while making it more difficult for companies to export products and services to the United States. Many economists and geopolitical analysts believe that if the euro remains high for an extended period of time, it may prompt fundamental changes on a variety of controversial policy issues including immigration laws, labor unions, and agricultural subsidies. It may also serve as a catalyst for Pan-European integration or prompt a wave of protectionism and isolation.

Asia's growth prospects are more of a mixed bag. In Japan, there seems to be no relief in sight for its economic woes. Its banks remain heavily in debt and in need of reform, its economy teeters on deflation, and its stock market continues to set 5- and 10-year lows. Growth in China, on the other hand, is booming. China is the world's largest recipient of foreign direct investment and is becoming an export powerhouse. Finally, India shows great potential for the long term and at some point could mirror China's economic miracle.

With respect to industry consolidation, the industrial mix among continents is also interesting. In Europe and Asia, for example, 15 percent of the industrial base falls into the opening stage of the Endgames Curve, with 45 percent, 30 percent, and 10 percent in the scale, focus, and balance and alliance stages, respectively. Compare these numbers to the U.S. industrial base, however, and a markedly different distribution image emerges. For example, 25 percent of U.S. companies are in the first stage, which suggests more favorable growth prospects. In addition, only

30 percent of the U.S. industrial base is in the scale stage, meaning that more national consolidation has already occurred. Finally, the United States has a higher weighting of balance and alliance stage companies, meaning that its companies have been slightly more successful at becoming global leaders in mature industries.

Growth Predictions in Key Industries

Scanning the business horizon industry by industry, we could make predictions all day. We start with a few interesting ones, and you can continue from there.

Pharmaceutical Industry

Throughout the 1990s, the pharmaceutical industry was a fairly staid and predictable industry (see Figure 13.2). Companies that invested heavily and steadily in R&D reaped the benefits of profitable new products and steadily rising share prices. Through the first half of the 1990s, Pfizer, for example, was a middle-tier competitor. Then, in 1994, Glaxo surprised its competitors by acquiring Burroughs Wellcome. In response, the Pfizer board and senior management team began to focus more carefully on growth and the industry's future landscape. They concluded that Pfizer needed to accelerate its growth engine to survive. The ensuing domino effect is striking.

Pfizer took a hard look at its R&D investments and began improving its ability to differentiate between winners and losers. One result was Viagra, one of the biggest winners in the history of the prescription drug industry. Pfizer dramatically upgraded the quality and effectiveness of its salesforce, teaching salespeople growth strategies and helping them focus on the biggest opportunities in the marketplace. Pfizer also embarked on a global expansion strategy. After surveying the competitive landscape, it made two bold acquisitions—Warner Lambert and Pharmacia. The result has been dramatic. From a has-been in the mid 1990s,

FIGURE 13.2   GLOBAL PHARMACEUTICAL INDUSTRY

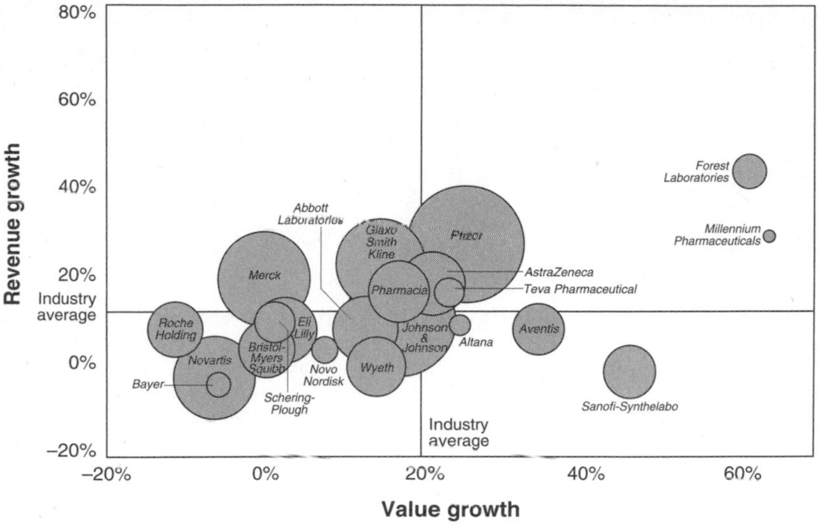

Note: Growth portfolio (CAGR 1997–2001) benchmarked against industry average.
Source: A.T. Kearney.

Pfizer has achieved an industry-leading 11 percent to 12 percent global market share, four percentage points ahead of the second largest player in the industry, GlaxoSmithKline, and seven percentage points ahead of Merck.

Pfizer shows no signs of stopping, either. Although valuations have fallen across the board in the industry, Pfizer seems poised to continue its acquisition rampage and pull even further away from the pack. Its competitors are left with two options: become bigger and stay within the range of parity with Pfizer or face extinction.

Automotive Industry

The automotive industry also faces an interesting future (see Figure 13.3). On one hand, its prospects for growth seem bright. Competitors such as BMW have produced exciting new models that consumers seem to want regardless of the price. Toyota continues

FIGURE 13.3   GLOBAL AUTOMOTIVE MANUFACTURERS
              INDUSTRY

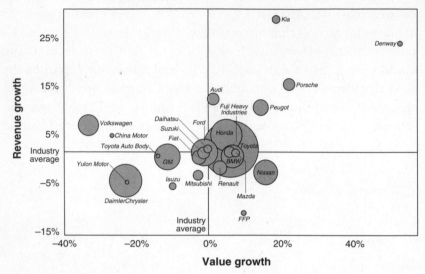

Note: Growth portfolio (CAGR 1997–2001) benchmarked against industry average.
Source: A.T. Kearney.

to grow organically, having aggressively entered Europe and expanded heavily in North America almost without competitive response. At the same time, some players are struggling. Daimler-Chrysler continues to face profitability challenges in the United States, in part because it is unable to make its Chrysler business unit profitable. GM and Ford face significant challenges from long-standing high-cost labor contracts and pension liabilities, as well as a saturated consumer market following heavy price discounting and low-cost financing programs after the September 11 events.

Two growth dynamics will shape the industry's future landscape: internal growth and acquisition. Companies that recommit to developing low-cost products that consumers want are almost certain to gain market share. Competitors would be wise to emulate the strategies of both Toyota and BMW or face an accelerating erosion of their market share. At the same time, M&A activity traditionally occurs in waves in the auto industry, the most recent being in Asia. The next wave of acquisitions seems destined to occur across the Atlantic Ocean, as more companies attempt to achieve the success that has proved elusive for DaimlerChrysler. Finally, warranty claims on vehicles sold with zero percent financing could pose a profit risk for U.S. OEMs in a few years. Within the next decade, we will undoubtedly see a significant shakeout in the automotive industry, with three or four strong, global, growth-oriented competitors emerging as the unquestioned leaders and several others exiting the industry either by choice or by fate.

Banking Industry

Consolidation has dominated the global banking industry for so long that it seems difficult to question a move away from that strategy (see Figure 13.4). However, the postmerger promises of *financial supermarkets* and growth through abundant cross-selling

FIGURE 13.4 GLOBAL BANKING INDUSTRY

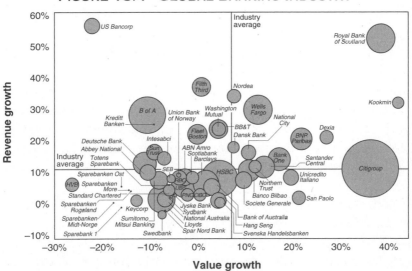

Note: Growth portfolio (CAGR 1997–2002) benchmarked against industry average.
Source: A.T. Kearney.

opportunities have proven elusive and have largely failed to create the next growth engine for the industry. At the same time, the power of processing technology has increased to the point at which new levels of economies of scale and globalization seem highly probable.

These dynamics present interesting possibilities for forecasting the future of the banking industry. Consolidation through the creation of financial utilities in the back-office functions of processing checks, payments, and loan approvals seems likely. A renewed focus on the core subindustries in the financial services industry will likely occur and be the basis for future growth, with diversified financial services supermarket companies likely divesting some of their diversified portfolios, slimming down, and returning to their roots. Finally, consolidation will continue, but this time at a cross-border level, both within Europe and across both oceans. Deals such as HSBC's acquisition of Household International and Citigroup's bid for Norisbank, the consumer lending division of Germany's HVB Group, are the prototypical cross-border banking mergers of the next decade. Imagine if the banking industry follows the consolidation and branding model of the retail industry, with an HSBC or Citigroup branch on every corner, right beside Starbucks and McDonald's.

The result of this upheaval will be a return to the roots for the industry. Delineation among commercial banks, consumer banks, leasing companies, brokerages, funds management companies, and all of the other financial services subindustries will become much clearer. This simplification should also enable senior executives to turn their attention to growth strategies.

STRETCH INTO THE FUTURE

We have now come full circle in the discussion of growth. Regardless of the state of the economy, the industry your company is in, and your current competitive position, growth opportunities abound. Growth may seem elusive at times, but if you begin by assessing operational improvements, follow through with organizational enhancements, conceive a strong growth strategy, and look for stretch growth opportunities, you will be successful.

Remember that the majority of successful companies attribute their success to execution. Achieving growth requires grit and attention to detail; competitive trench warfare will be the determining factor in your success. Get ready to roll up your sleeves and prepare your management team and your whole company to work on the fundamentals.

It all begins with a first step. With this in mind, we exhort you to seize the moment and start work on a growth strategy for your company today.

Overview of Economic Value Added (EVA) and Other Value Frameworks

EVA will never be able to explain why Bill Gates embraces the Internet.

The Economist, August 2, 1997

The most popular tool used in finance today is the discounted cash flow (DCF) method, which is the sum of the company's current and future discounted cash flows. The number is not an easy one to calculate, however, because of the various pieces of information it requires, including estimates of future cash flows.

In recent years, a number of companies have turned to alternative valuation techniques because they generate short-term successes. Cases in point: cash flow return on investment (CFROI) and EVA, created by consultancy Stern Stewart.

The EVA metric, in general, is the surplus value of the after-tax operating profit after deducting all cost of doing business, including the cost of debt and the opportunity cost of equity. The exact calculation, as defined by its founders, is somewhat more complicated:

$$\text{EVA} = \left(\begin{array}{c} \text{Return on} \\ \text{capital invested} \end{array} - \begin{array}{c} \text{Cost of} \\ \text{capital} \end{array} \right) \times \begin{array}{c} \text{Capital} \\ \text{invested} \end{array}$$

Capital invested is also a challenging calculation. Normally, it requires book value that is undergoing numerous adjustments:

- Capitalizing operating expenses that are really financing expenses in disguise
- Eliminating any items that may cause book value of capital to drop without having a significant impact on capital invested (e.g., restructuring charges)
- Adjusting for actions that should have caused book value of capital to fall but did not because of accounting treatment

$$\text{Return on capital} = \frac{\text{Operating income}\,(1 - \text{tax rate})}{\text{Capital invested}}$$

two main adjustments made:

1. R&D adjustment: EBIT (earnings before and taxes) + R&D expenses
2. Operating lease adjustment: EBIT + Operating lease expenses

Cost of capital : WACC (weighted average cost of capital) : Weighting the cost for debt and equity

When comparing different value methods and value drivers, a number of indicators can be used to determine the effectiveness of a certain framework in generating value for the company and its stockholders. Following are the four main indicators:

1. *The value method can be disaggregated.* This indicator is used to calculate for the whole company, including business units. The main reason stock price-related measures such as market capitalization (MC), adjusted market capitalization (AMC), and total shareholder returns (TSR) are considered defective is that they can hardly be disaggregated and used on a subcompany level. Yet, most companies today are large and comprise a portfolio of different business units. To steer them effectively, the management team needs ratios on the subcompany level—here DCF, EVA, CFROI, and profit ratios such as EBIT and EBITDA (earnings before interest, taxes, depreciation, and amortization) growth are much more effective.

In addition, incentive systems should be linked to the creation of value. In many cases, it is necessary to disaggregate incentive systems to a subcompany level to create a meaningful incentive system. An employee of a small business unit has practically no effect on the overall performance of a large company. Therefore, it is not efficient or wise to create incentives based on the stock price. For employees, the incentive is like gambling in Las Vegas— their work has no effect on the odds. It is much better to link the incentive or bonus to a goal that employees can actively influence.

2. *The theoretical exactness of the value framework.* There are essentially three levers that influence the value of the company. First, the static value of the company can be increased. Second, the expected growth rate can be boosted. Third, the cost of capital can be reduced. DCF, EVA, and CFROI measure all three components, while profit ratios cover only static value and expected growth rates.

3. *Practicability.* Whether the calculation is practical is another important indicator of the effectiveness of a value framework. Are the indicators easy to calculate? Do they build on existing accounting systems? Are they easy to communicate (for incentive

systems)? Here, profit ratios score high while DCF, CFROI, and especially EVA show significant problems. Operational managers in most cases simply desert the financial literacy that is necessary to understand and implement EVA in their day-to-day business. And maybe this is simply not their job.

4. *Benchmarking.* For strategic reasons, it is important to compare the performance of your company with that of your direct or indirect competitors. Stock prices are easy to benchmark—the same holds true for profit ratios. Because the modern value ratios are more difficult to calculate, benchmarking is not as easy (see Figure A.1).

Recently, more users of the EVA concept have awakened to find that the effects of implementation have worn off. Or worse, sometimes it seems that short-term success was bought at the expense of long-term growth opportunities, thereby lowering the company value rather than increasing it. Besides the advantages that many

FIGURE A.1 PROFITABLE VERSUS NONPROFITABLE CUSTOMERS

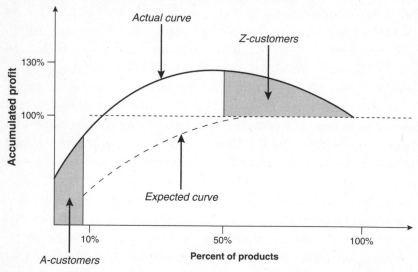

Source: A.T. Kearney.

EVA implementations can offer, namely incentive systems and a certain focus on growth (although neither is actually a unique achievement of EVA), EVA also has a significant drawback—it encourages managers to keep the capital invested low to increase EVA. Therefore, after a couple of years, the innovation and investment pipeline dries up and the growth of the company recedes. It may bring further attractive profits for a year or two, but from a strategic point of view, the company has just driven down a dead-end street.

Therefore, from a measurement and incentive perspective, EVA has some major drawbacks. Managers either don't understand the concept at all, they understand the concept and use it to their advantage (thereby sacrificing long-term benefit), or they understand the concept and don't differ from the long-term benefit of the company, contrary to what EVA says.

(On the theoretical problems of EVA, see also Aswath Damodaran's paper *Value Creation and Enhancement* [New York University, Leonard N. Stern School Finance Department Working Paper Series, 1999]. The economic value added approach yields the same value as a DCF valuation, and it requires more information, which is especially difficult to obtain when using EVA at the subdivisional level.)

PRICING STRATEGIES

Companies that look at three categories—product management, customer management, and assortment management—can assess their own standing in assortments and pricing to find and then fill potential gaps. Ideally, you should view the three categories as phases or stages of excellence. The majority of companies today have already captured the information needed to reach the first stage of excellence, or product management, while many other companies are well into the second stage, customer management. Insurance companies (Progressive auto insurer) and banks (Deutsche Bank) in particular are traditionally strong in managing customer accounts. Only a handful of companies, if that, have moved beyond this second stage to arrive at the assortment management stage. The following offers our perspective on the three stages of excellence.

Product Management

Mainstream product management information remains the most widely used tool. It includes important methods such as activity-based costing (ABC) analysis for segmenting products, margin analysis, different ratios on price analysis, and product life cycle analysis.

Product management tools can help companies answer key questions such as: Which products are profitable? Which generate the biggest revenues? Which products should we focus on? What is the optimal price for a product as a stand-alone offering? Which products are the stars of tomorrow—and what investments should be discontinued?

Product management is critical when introducing new offerings. Even renowned companies sometimes miss the mark as they search for the right introductory price level. Volkswagen's new Beetle and P&G's Charmin toilet paper are both examples of initial overpricing.

Sometimes this miscalculation results from errors in market research. For instance, consumers may be shown a product and asked whether they would buy it at certain prices. Unfortunately, this type of experiment fails to replicate reality. In practice, the consumer has the option to buy the new product—or competing ones—depending on price. By omitting comparison products, the experiment generally overestimates the price level the market will bear.

Although it's an important management tool, a simple product view of pricing fails to account for the link between different products and services of an assortment, especially in industries that do not sell single products to their customers. When customers buy a basket of products and services, a company decision that targets isolated products will affect other products in the process. It's not hard to imagine potential scenarios in which a company inadvertently eliminates a loss leader that was drawing new customers to its store.

Despite the popularity of simple product pricing tools, companies recognize the need to assess product interdependencies. Businesses are also finding that as it becomes easier to replicate products and services, it also becomes more difficult to maintain cost leadership. And advantages gained by investing in advanced technologies rarely remain proprietary over the long term. These marketplace realities have prompted management to move beyond a pure product view to a more customer-focused perspective. Customer relationship management (CRM), designed to attract and retain the most profitable customers, helps companies cope with the problems of isolated product management.

Customer Management

Advances in information technology have made it much easier to leverage customer information. New tools such as customer cards and scanner data help to capture more information. Data warehouses offer new ways to store it. Faster algorithms analyze it in record time. The emergence of e-commerce as a sales channel enforces this trend and has created a strong demand for e-CRM solution packages from companies including Siebel System, Broad Vision, and Oracle.

CRM accounting is a useful tactic that uses customer information to calculate ratios such as revenue by customer, margin by customer, and lifetime value of customers.[1] Yet, overhyped CRM analyses can sometimes overestimate the value of the customer. For example, you can sum up your lifetime values at a few favorite companies where you shop regularly—and quickly arrive at values that exceed your actual lifetime income, at least what you expect to earn in a lifetime.

Using CRM, companies are able to answer key questions. Which clients are the most profitable—and how do we retain them? How can we attract more customers? Can we cross-sell our offerings?

Companies can benefit from customer management via a simple calculation of profit by customer. This analysis often results in an ABCZ curve—that is, there are not only customers that deliver small profits, but also customers that for periods of time do not bring in any profit at all and are not strategic customers.

Examples abound of companies that have successfully used customer management to increase the profitability of their assortments, including Capital One, First Direct, Tesco, and Orange. But there have also been failures because this type of customer management can be expensive and time consuming. Asda and Safeway, two British retailers, recently eliminated their loyalty reward systems because they were no longer attracting customers and were not gathering useful data.

Another issue with customer management is that although many companies can collect data, they find it difficult to act on the information. Political or psychological considerations may persuade them not to reject a customer whose basket of goods yields too low a margin or not to charge customer-specific prices when all the data says they should.

Customer management is highly related to a dynamic pricing technique known as yield management. Yield management maximizes sales and profits by determining optimal prices; it is particularly beneficial in industries with perishable products and services. A key concept behind yield management is price discrimination by customer segments. The airline industry is arguably the best example, based on, for instance, when a flight is booked. Price-sensitive customers book early, well in advance of a flight, while business customers and those who are willing to pay more tend to wait until they really need the service before they book a flight.

Yield management is designed to adjust prices in such a way that demand and supply are always aligned. With a set of yield management tools based on mathematical operations research modeling, American Airlines is among the most prominent examples of how to successfully implement the yield management concept.

Assortment Management

The third logical step in pricing excellence is assortment management, which deals with questions such as: What is the optimal complexity of the assortment? Which products are profitable when interdependencies are considered? Which products should be added to or deleted from the assortment? What is the optimal price for one product as part of an assortment? Which products are the stars of tomorrow, and what investments should be discontinued?

Today, most business-to-consumer companies are managing assortments of several thousand products and services. The complexity of assortments continues to increase dramatically. The management of such mega-assortments is a challenge, due not only to sheer size, but also to the flexibility required, because assortment management must adapt to changing customer needs and tastes.

Assortment management is a crucial task. Even small alterations of the composition of the assortment or the pricing of some key products can make or break a company. Consider Toys 'R Us, which successfully expanded geographically, but stumbled when it waited too long to change its assortment from traditional toys to electronic games.

Think of a typical retail decision—whether to offer a loss leader. Judging a loss leader by its sales almost always results in a positive evaluation; conducting the same evaluation with profits as the key metric would yield the opposite result. In other words, indicators such as sales and profits are basically useless in determining the success of a loss leader. The key purpose of a loss leader is to bring in customers who buy the loss leader as well as other more profitable products. If that happens, the loss leader strategy has worked; if most customers buy only the loss leader, the special sale will prove disastrous.

Therefore, the success of products within an assortment can be measured by determining conjoint profits.[2] Conjoint profits are determined as follows:

1. Calculate the margin of every customer's basket of goods.

2. For every basket, determine the share of a certain product in the overall basket (in terms of sales). This figure is the allocation key.

3. Use the allocation key to reallocate the margin of the basket of goods to the products.

4. Add all of the reallocated basket margins in which this product was included to determine the overall conjoint profit for a product.

Conjoint profits (not to be confused with conjoint measurement techniques) reveal the total profit impact of a single product within an assortment.

The three groups of pricing tools discussed here can generate useful information. How they are used depends on the industry and its unique products and customers. In many cases, it will be necessary to tailor product and pricing systems to best meet your needs based on the nature of the business, the volume of data, and the information. The best solution for any company is to combine these various tools, emphasizing those that are the most relevant to your business sector and company environment.

For example, assortment management tools are extremely helpful in sectors with large assortments that have strong interdependencies among different products, such as retail, insurance, banking, telecom, transportation, tourism, and leisure. In classic business-to-business industries, the interdependencies between products and services are not as strong, and product and customer management techniques are more important.

NOTES

CHAPTER SIX

1. For more information, see www.itw.com/80_20/about_80_20 .html.

CHAPTER SEVEN

1. Securities and Exchange Commission Form 10-K for Graco, 2002.

CHAPTER EIGHT

1. www.gs.com.

CHAPTER TEN

1. The Basic Nestlé Management and Leadership Principles, Section 4, www.nestle.com.

APPENDIX

1. Robert C. Blattberg and J. Deighton, "Manage Marketing by the Customer Equity," *Harvard Business Review,* no. 4 (1996).

2. P. Recht and S. Zeisel, "Retail Pricing with Conjoint Profits," *Diskussionsbeiträge des Fachgebietes Operations Research und Wirtschaftsinformatik,* nr. 14 (University of Dortmund, 1999).

INDEX